FOUR CENTURIES

OF FURNITURE

IN PORTSMOUTH

Four Centuries of

FURNITURE
IN PORTSMOUTH

with the
NEW HAMPSHIRE FURNITURE MASTERS

GERALD W. R. WARD

with the Assistance of
Hollis Brodrick and **Lainey McCartney**

Portsmouth Marine Society Publication 38
Portsmouth Historical Society
Portsmouth, New Hampshire

2017

Published on the occasion of an exhibition held in the Academy Gallery
at the
Discover Portsmouth Center, Portsmouth, New Hampshire
April 7–June 18, 2017
© 2017 Portsmouth Historical Society

FRONTISPIECE:
High chest of drawers, Joseph Davis (w. 1726–62), Portsmouth, 1735–45,
Walnut, walnut veneer, eastern white pine, H. 75¼ in., W. 48¼ in., D.
25¼ in., Private collection. *(See cat. no. 17)*

PRE TITLE PAGE:
Detail, Box, Hampton, New Hampshire, area, 1670–1700, Eastern white
pine, H. 9 in., W. 23¾ in., D. 16¾ in. Private collection. *(See cat. no. 2)*

PORTSMOUTH MARINE SOCIETY
PORTSMOUTH HISTORICAL SOCIETY
P.O. BOX 728
PORTSMOUTH, NEW HAMPSHIRE 03802

DESIGN: SUSAN KRESS HAMILTON, PHINEAS GRAPHICS
PORTSMOUTH, NEW HAMPSHIRE

PRINTING: PENMOR LITHOGRAPHERS
LEWISTON, MAINE

Library of Congress Cataloging-in-Publication Data

Names: Ward, Gerald W. R., author. | Portsmouth Historical Society, issuing
    body. | New Hampshire Furniture Masters Association.
Title: Four centuries of furniture in Portsmouth, with the New Hampshire
    Furniture Masters / Gerald W.R. Ward ; with the assistance of Hollis
    Brodrick and Lainey McCartney.
Description: Portsmouth, New Hampshire : Portsmouth Historical Society, 2017.
    | Series: Portsmouth Marine Society publication ; 38 | "Published on the
    occasion of an exhibition held in the Academy Gallery at the Discover
    Portsmouth Center, Portsmouth, New Hampshire April 7-June 18, 2017." |
    Includes bibliographical references.
Identifiers: LCCN 2017011640 | ISBN 9780915819454 (alk. paper)
Subjects: LCSH: Furniture--New Hampshire--Portsmouth--Exhibitions. | Studio
    furniture--New England--Exhibitions.
Classification: LCC NK2438.P67 W37 2017 | DDC 749.09742/6--dc23
LC record available at https://lccn.loc.gov/2017011640

LENDERS TO THE EXHIBITION

Robert L. Barth

Ronald Bourgeault

Hollis Brodrick

Dr. Peter Brown and
Ms. Blair Weaver

Robert Chase and Richard Candee

Charles B. Doleac Collection

Thomas P. Hand, Sr.

Andrew Hanzlian

Claudia Hopf and Perry Hopf

Craig and Alison Jewett

Moffatt-Ladd House & Garden

Douglas Nelson and
Karin Cullity Nelson

New Hampshire Furniture Masters
Association

New Hampshire Historical Society

Portsmouth Athenaeum

Portsmouth Historical Society

Michael and Gloria Reopel

Strawbery Banke Museum

Peter Vocca

Warner House Association

Michael V. Wise

and

several private collections

Contents.

ABOVE: Desk box, Portsmouth or Kittery, Maine, ca. 1685, Oak, pine, H. 7¾ in., W. 16⅛ in., D. 11 in., Private collection. *(See cat. no. 1)*

Sponsors:

SEASON

Rotary Club of Portsmouth
Portsmouth Painting Company

EXHIBITION

Mr. & Mrs. Craig Jewett, and the Jewett Family

Ronald Bourgeault
Hollis Brodrick

Antiques & Fine Art Magazine

Peter Eaton
Donald Koleman & Joanna Brode Koleman
Mr. & Mrs. David McCartney
The Charles S. Parsons Fund
Peter Sawyer Antiques
Aileen Dugan-State Farm Insurance
Jonathan & Susan Paige Trace
Gary F. Yeaton

Melissa Alden & Jack Kane, and Sharon Platt
Bernard & S. Dean Levy, Inc.
Nathan Liverant and Son Antiques
The Meader Family
Doug Nelson/Wells Fargo Advisors, LLC
New Hampshire Antiques Dealers Association

The exhibition catalogue has been generously underwritten
by Mr. & Mrs. Craig Jewett, and the Jewett Family.

Foreword.

IN 2016, the Portsmouth Historical Society mounted two principal exhibitions in our Academy Gallery. We first featured the paintings and other works by the American impressionist painter Edmund C. Tarbell, as well as a complementary show of works by contemporary members of the Tarbell school. This exhibition was followed by a retrospective show of the extraordinary contemporary art of Wendy Turner from Kittery Point. This year, we have shifted our focus from two-dimensional works of art to those of three dimensions, beginning with this brief survey of four centuries of furniture in Portsmouth, to be followed by a look at three important Seacoast sculptors.

The phrase "furniture *in* Portsmouth" recognizes our role as a history museum, in that we are taking a look here at objects with important Portsmouth histories as well as ones made by local artisans and artists. We are proud to showcase the Seacoast's heritage of locally made and owned furniture from the seventeenth century to the present on the first floor of our space, while displaying on the second floor a companion show of masterworks by the New Hampshire Furniture Masters Association, an organization of outstanding contemporary studio furniture makers. These dual presentations follow our emerging tradition of interpreting and exhibiting both the past and the present.

As with all such projects, "Four Centuries of Furniture in Portsmouth" required the efforts of many people. I am particularly grateful to the show's curator, Gerry Ward, and his principal collaborators: Lainey McCartney, Curatorial Associate; Jeffrey Cooper, chair of the Furniture Masters; and Hollis Brodrick of Portsmouth, who has generously volunteered his time and provided his expertise in early local material. Every member of our staff has contributed to various aspects of this project, including Judy Loto, Cynthia Novotny, Erika Beer, Wendy Rolfe, Robin Lurie-Meyerkopf, Robin Albert, Claire Spollen, Jessica Kliskey, Maddy Shuldmanour, our intern Elizabeth Robinson, and our former staff member Allison Galliher. Richard Candee developed the idea for this show several years ago and has been instrumental in seeing it through to completion. Our board, members, and volunteers, especially our Events Committee, are crucial to all that we do. We are also particularly grateful to the many public and private lenders, listed elsewhere, who have made their objects available to us. In particular, I would like to thank many of our sister institutions in Portsmouth who have been unfailingly helpful when called upon. Susan Kress Hamilton of Phineas Graphics has once again lent her considerable skills to the design of this catalogue and the exhibition graphics.

Essential funding for this publication has been provided by Craig and Alison Jewett. Their support of our endeavors is greatly appreciated. We are also grateful to our many other supporters who have made the installation possible.

Furniture—in common with all types of objects—offers a window into the attitudes and values of people in both the past and the present. The objects presented here are tangible reminders of the daily lives of their owners and the artistic aspirations of their makers. As the celebration of the city's four hundredth anniversary approaches in 2023, we are proud to present this snapshot of one aspect of our Seacoast area's distinctive material life, in both high style and vernacular expressions.

KATHLEEN SOLDATI
Executive Director
Portsmouth Historical Society

Detail, Armchair, England, 1680–90, Beech, H. 48¼ in., S.W.14½ in., S.D. 16¼ in., Strawbery Banke Museum; Gift of Old Colony Historical Society (1992.17). *(See cat. no. 3)*

Introduction.

FOR MANY YEARS, Portsmouth's early furniture had been of interest to collectors, curators, and connoisseurs, but it did not receive the attention afforded to the products of colonial America's larger urban centers. The nascent study of the subject coalesced in a major exhibition entitled "Portsmouth Furniture: Masterworks from the New Hampshire Seacoast," organized by Brock Jobe and the Society for the Preservation of New England Antiquities (now Historic New England) in 1992, accompanied by a substantial catalogue published in 1993. Based on detailed research by a cadre of scholars led by Jobe, that project resulted in one of the landmark studies in the literature on American furniture. This much more modest effort is an homage to that work, now about a quarter of a century old, and is clearly indebted to it at nearly every step. Our exhibition brings to light some objects that have emerged or been acquired by institutions since 1992, while revisiting a few of the great pieces that were featured in the earlier effort. While following in many of the same footsteps, we have departed from its path by extending the time span under consideration by including objects made after 1825 and a few utilitarian, vernacular, or even quirky objects. We have also placed a little more emphasis on objects *owned* in Portsmouth, as well as those *made* here, a necessity due to our interest in the late nineteenth and twentieth centuries. And we are also presenting a corollary exhibition featuring works by the New Hampshire Furniture Masters Association, in keeping with the Portsmouth Historical Society's efforts to make our exhibitions contemporary as well as historical in nature. One last word of introduction: Our title is borrowed from another effort led by Jobe, a recent multi-year celebration by eleven institutions of "Four Centuries of Massachusetts Furniture."

The predominant furniture style in Portsmouth in 2017 might be called "contemporary utilitarian." In a little city of only some 21,000 residents that has 2,200 hotel rooms (with more to come) and some 23,000 restaurant seats, how could it be otherwise? Such modern versions of "borax" furniture (as it used to be called) are typically made overseas in China or Southeast Asia, although some might be American.

Portsmouth's domestic consumers have a wider range of choice. The town supports a number of fine retail establishments and outlets—Cabot House, Ethan Allen, Allen's Wayside Furniture, Furniture Forever, Adobe, and sections of various department stores—that provide mass-market goods of varying levels for consumers. With the internet, of course, citizens have access to goods of all kinds worldwide. Many exercise that option. Some, for example, furnish their homes *(cat. no. 50)* or remodel their kitchens with IKEA products, a popular brand with the younger generations.

At the other end of the spectrum, Portsmouth and the immediate area are also home to several studio furniture makers, among them Matt Wajda of River City Furnituremaking *(fig. 1)*, David Masury of Kittery Point, Maine,

Thomas P. Hand, Sr., of Rye *(cat. no. 49)*, George Beland, and William Clarke. Jeffrey Cooper *(cat. no. 48)* also works in Portsmouth and is currently chair of the New Hampshire Furniture Masters. These and a few other makers keep the area's longstanding tradition of woodworking alive and well as we approach the city's four-hundredth anniversary in 2023, but they are in the minority.

How did we reach this situation of a predominantly retail market supplemented by extraordinary survivals of handcraftsmanship? The central role of imported furniture sold at retail is not a new phenomenon in Portsmouth or most other small towns. The key figures in the furniture trade since

Fig.1. Matt Wajda (b. 1970), pair of card tables, Portsmouth, 2006.
Mahogany, holly, ebony, and avodire veneers, oil varnish finish;
H. 28 in., W. 36 in., D. closed 18 in.
Private collection, Wellesley, Massachusetts.

about 1850 have been retail establishments, as improved transportation and communication networks made it easier for large factories to sell their goods to a wide audience. In 1905, chairs and tables *(cat. nos. 46A–46C)* needed for the peace treaty negotiations held in Portsmouth to conclude the Russo-Japanese war were purchased from W.B. Moses and Son, a prolific manufacturer in Washington, D.C. The Portsmouth Furniture Company, which sold off the peace treaty materials after the conclusion of the negotiations, was located at the corner of Deer and Vaughan streets and billed themselves as the "Largest House Furnishing Establishment in the State." The long-lived retailer Margeson Brothers similarly supplied furniture in various styles *(cat. nos. 46, 47)* to local citizens, using stenciled or paper labels to identify their wares. One notable local carver of the late nineteenth and early twentieth century, John Haley Bellamy, turned his hand occasionally to furniture, but is best known for his impressive eagles that formed the basis for a major exhibition at the Portsmouth Historical Society in 2014.

The sale of the peace treaty furniture reminds us of the longstanding importance of recycled furniture in the local market. Estate auctions and vendues in the eighteenth and nineteenth century were popular ways for people to acquire furniture, allowing them on occasion to get a bargain but also clouding the "family history" that accompanies many objects. The noted antiques dealer Charles "Cappy" Stewart and the nineteenth-century newspaperman Charles W. Brewster, responsible for many of Portsmouth's most-loved stories *(see cat. no. 3)*, helped foster a market for antiques in the nineteenth century. Today, Portsmouth is home to outstanding collectors of and dealers in Americana, several of whom are represented in this exhibition, and is the location of Northeast Auctions, operated by the legendary Ron Bourgeault.

As Portsmouth began to wane as a furniture-making center, local historic house museums and societies started to collect and preserve Portsmouth's heritage, including furniture, a process that is now more than century old and is ongoing. Historic New England, the Warner House Association *(cat. no. 15)*, Strawbery Banke Museum *(cat. no. 16)*, the Portsmouth Athenaeum *(cat. no. 22)*, the Moffatt-Ladd House & Garden *(cat. nos. 24B, 25–28)*, and other local organizations, as well as the Portsmouth Historical Society, care for and display some of the city's finest early furniture as well as some of its more vernacular *(cat. nos. 40, 42–44)* and unusual *(cat. no. 41)* examples.

The older families in the area, such as the Wendell family, in the best New England fashion simply "had their things." An important but usually overlooked subset of craftsmen who played a significant role in Portsmouth's furniture history includes individuals who restored the possessions and antiques owned by these families. John H. Stickney and George Fernald were two early furniture "conservators" who, on at least several occasions, signed and dated their repairs in the late nineteenth and early twentieth centuries.

Fig. 2. Samuel Dockum (1792–1872), unidentified artist, probably Portsmouth, ca. 1840. Oil on yellow-poplar board; H. 38⅝ in., W. 33½ in. including frame. Portsmouth Historical Society; Gift of Serena Jones (463).

Samuel Dockum's career spanned from the 1820s to the 1860s *(fig. 2)*. He is representative of the successors to the city's colonial and federal-period woodworking traditions who, in some ways, saw it come to an end. As the research of Johanna McBrien has shown, Dockum's grand plan for a lucrative career was dashed by the Panic of 1837. He may even have turned his hand to repairs. In the 1840s, Sarah Parker Rice Goodwin acquired an early daybed of ca. 1700 and briefly considered having Dockum repair it. However, Ichabod Goodwin, her husband, forbade it. Dockum, he said, "would knock it to pieces & think it only fit to be burned."

Fig. 3. Langley Boardman (1774-1833),
possibly by Ethan Allen Greenwood (1779–1856),
Portsmouth, 1800–1810. Oil on canvas;
H. 31½ in. W. 27⅞ in.
Portsmouth Historical Society;
Gift of Frances Tredick (277).

of high-style cabinetmaking by the third quarter of the nineteenth century.

Langley Boardman *(see fig. 3)* and the firm of Jonathan Judkins and William Senter *(cat. no.28)* were among Dockum's most illustrious predecessors in the federal period and may well have been his career models. Portsmouth furniture in the 1790 to 1820 period is a notable regional contribution to an American aesthetic. Although closely related to the furniture of eastern Massachusetts, Portsmouth furniture speaks with something of an individual accent, notable for its use in case furniture of striking color contrasts achieved through the skillful use of light and dark flitches of birch and mahogany veneers. Although many objects were imported, including fancy painted side chairs, Portsmouth remained a viable cabinetmaking center during a period of population growth (from 4,720 in 1790 to 7,320 in 1820). Fluctuating economic circumstances, as always, affected the

Although he continued in business *(see cat. nos. 35, 38)*, as did Samuel P. Treadwell *(cat. no. 36)*, Edmund P. Brown *(cat. nos. 37A, 37B)* and others, Dockum's Portsmouth had become something of a backwater in terms

market, and the era was punctuated by devastating downtown fires, particularly in 1813. These fires led to a substantial rebuilding in brick, and they may have led a significant number of Portsmouth residents to brand their furniture *(see fig. 4)* for identification purposes. This practice presumably was helpful to the owners of the objects at the time and has proven to be an asset for

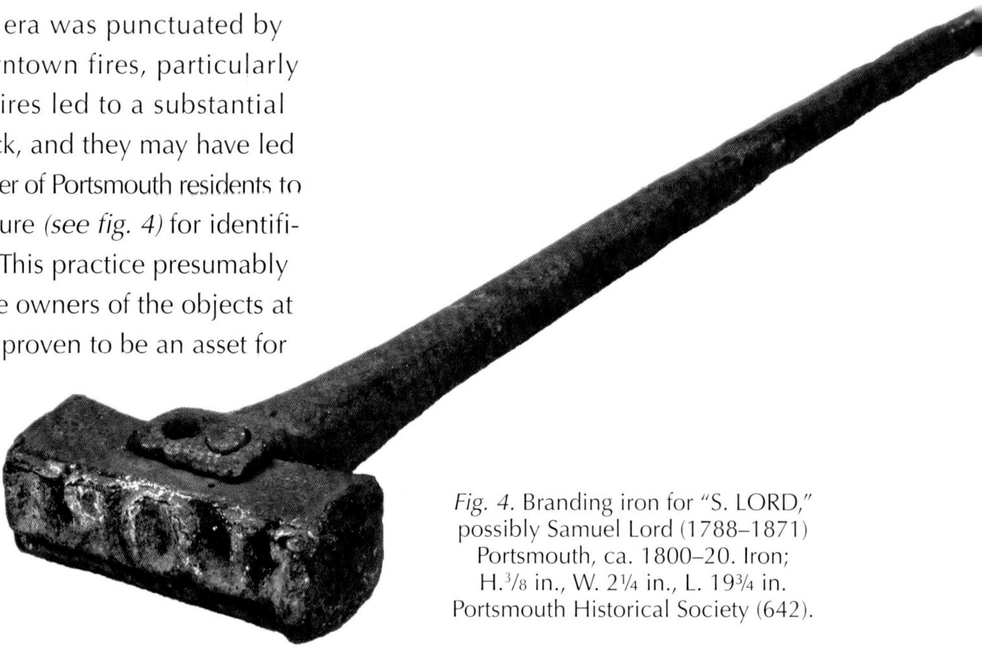

Fig. 4. Branding iron for "S. LORD," possibly Samuel Lord (1788–1871) Portsmouth, ca. 1800–20. Iron; H.$^3/_8$ in., W. 2$^1/_4$ in., L. 19$^3/_4$ in. Portsmouth Historical Society (642).

modern furniture collectors and scholars seeking to identify local work *(see cat. nos. 29A–29B, 30A–30B)*.

Often likened even today to an English seaport town, Portsmouth in the decades before the American Revolution was a provincial maritime community in the Anglo-American Atlantic world. Its principal cabinetmaker in the decade before hostilities was an English-born and trained artisan named Robert Harrold *(see cat. nos. 25, 34A)*. He put his aesthetic stamp on the most "modern" furniture in town, borrowing designs from English pattern books and employing English decorative modes and construction techniques. His work is a good reminder of the important of immigrants to all phases of American life. Its inherent "Englishness" is also a reminder that colonial Americans considered themselves Englishmen in the 1760s and 1770s, and that their rebellion was aimed at re-gaining the traditional rights they had enjoyed since the time of Magna Carta in 1215. They were, as the inscription on Paul Revere's Sons of Liberty bowl reminds us, "undaunted by the insolent menaces of villains in power" (namely George III and Parliament) and determined to regain what was their due as English subjects.

Harrold, when he arrived in Portsmouth in 1765, landed in a town that had been settled by immigrants for more than a century. In the second and third quarters of the eighteenth century, the seaport had largely been a prosperous community, at least for some. Magnificent Georgian dwellings such as the brick Archibald Macphaedris house (1716) and the John Langdon mansion (1784) serve as bookends to this era, with the extraordinary house built by John Moffatt in 1761–63 standing in the middle of this period. John Drew, Joseph Davis (cat. nos. 16, 17), John Gaines III (cat. no. 19), and many others supplied furniture to local customers, in styles that echoed—and can be hard to distinguish from—the work produced in Boston, Salem, and other towns in the Massachusetts Bay Colony. Chairmaking, not only for local customers but for export up and down the coast, as far away as Newfoundland, was an important staple of local turners and chairmakers. Examples of their banister- back chairs and other forms are liberally represented in this exhibition. The best of these chairs, such as cat. no. 9, are bold, abstract designs enriched with embellishments. The carved crest of this chair, with its leafage, scrolls, and notching, is an outstanding passage. One local variant, found in prolific numbers in the area (cat. nos. 11A–11C), sports a peculiar crest rail often referred to as a "fish-tail." As Phil Zea noted, these popular chairs have "paired fish tails perpetually poised for a dive into the briny deep." Case furniture from the William and Mary period (ca. 1690–1730) from the area remains largely unidentified, although it surely was made here. But by about 1715, Portsmouth had entered a period marked by increasing Georgian grace and gentility.

Although Portsmouth was founded in 1623, furniture from the first century of settlement has not survived in great quantities. Only a few houses—the Richard Jackson house (ca. 1644 and later) owned by Historic New England and the Sherburne house (ca. 1695 and later) preserved by Strawbery Banke, along with some of the woodwork from the John Wentworth house (ca. 1695–1700, now installed as a period room at the Metropolitan Museum of Art)—remain to represent the seventeenth century. Furniture from this early period is nearly as scarce. A remarkable armchair (cat. no. 4), probably made in the Boston area and owned by the Burnham family of Durham from its creation until 2015, is a rare exception. An English chair (cat. no. 3) is also thought to have a venerable history in the area in the Fernald family; it is one of a few English first-period objects with local histories to survive. To find other early furniture made in the Seacoast region, one has to expand the circle to include the Hampton area *(see cat. nos. 2, 6)*.

A handful of pieces made in the 1680s can be traced to a Portsmouth craftsman (or possibly one across the river in Kittery). That group is represented here by a small desk box *(cat. no. 1)* that exhibits carved motifs very similar to those found on the other three surviving members of the group. The maker was probably an immigrant from the West Country of England or was trained by someone from that area of the mother country. His work and the other remnants from this earliest period remind us that the first immigrants sought, in their furniture and architecture, to replicate forms and designs they had known in England.

As this catalogue was coming to completion, a remarkable little table *(cat. no. 23)* was given to the Portsmouth Historical Society by Anne and Alan Cutter. While unappealing to most furniture collectors— two of its legs are replaced and the top has been reduced in size—its traditional history raises it from simply a prosaic table to a profound document. Family history and several inscriptions relate that it was given by Sir William Pepperrell to his slave, Molly Miles. Although such a provenance can be difficult to prove, this one is almost as well corroborated as one could wish. As the research of Patricia Q. Wall demonstrates, Molly Miles was one of several hundred African Americans who resided in the Seacoast area from the early seventeenth century but whose existence, up until recently, was lived "below the level of historical scrutiny." Modest as it is, "Molly's Table" sheds light on the daily life and circumstances of its owner. It stands in contrast to the more high-style objects that museums and collectors tend to covet, especially those that retain their original feet, glue blocks, old brasses, and all those other beloved details. But it is perhaps even a more powerful embodiment of memory, allowing us to imagine, or at least to conjecture, what life must have been like for those who did not participate in the tea drinking, card playing, and fine dining characteristic of gentry life in the Piscataqua region in the mid eighteenth century. As such, it also reminds us that furniture—objects most of us use every day in our lives—can be interpreted in many ways, as documents of social history, as examples of craftsmanship and changing technology, but perhaps most importantly as tangible reminders of specific individuals and evocations of their memory.

GERALD W. R. WARD

The Catalogue.

Unless otherwise noted, the dimensions given here are overall or "outside" dimensions. Woods and other materials have been identified by eye or are based on information provided by the lender. Entries prepared in large part by Hollis Brodrick are indicated by the initials HB. For additional information, see the Note on Sources at the back of this book. We are particularly indebted to the work of several scholars in *Portsmouth Furniture: Masterworks from the New Hampshire Seacoast,* edited and organized by Brock Jobe and published by the Society for the Preservation of New England Antiquities (now Historic New England) in Boston in 1993, and referred to in these entries by the short title *Portsmouth Furniture.*

Ambrotype of Civil War soldier, ca. 1860s.
Private collection.

1 DESK BOX
Portsmouth or Kittery, Maine, ca. 1685
Oak, pine
H. 7¾ in., W. 16⅛ in., D. 11 in.
Private collection

Although the Portsmouth area was settled in the early seventeenth century, very little furniture from the first decades of immigrant life survives. This recently discovered small desk box is thus of major importance. It is only the fourth member of a small group of carved furniture dating from the mid-1680s to be identified. It joins a chest at the Museum of Fine Arts, Boston, with the carved date of 1685 and the initials "RS"; a chest at the Virginia Museum of Fine Arts, dated 1684 and with the initials "IW," that descended in the Treadwell and Williams families of Portsmouth; and a third, unpublished chest (private collection). With a sloping pine top and oak sides and front, the desk box is of nailed-board construction. The distinctive carving on the front panel of the desk box shares many of the same motifs and appears to be by the same hand that carved the other three pieces. The furniture scholar Robert F. Trent has linked these chests in terms of their style and construction to furniture made in Gloucestershire, in the West Country of England.

2 BOX
Hampton, New Hampshire, area, 1670–1700
Eastern white pine
H. 9 in., W. 23¾ in., D 16¾ in.
Private collection

This box is part of a small group of seventeenth-century board chests and boxes linked to the same shop in Hampton, New Hampshire. Three examples in this group retain histories, respectively, in the Marston, Batchelder, and Fogg families of that town. Russell Hawes Kettell, in *The Pine Furniture of Early New England* (1929), was the first author to give a detailed description of a chest and to link it with this area: his chest was "found in a barn in Hampton, New Hampshire" (pp. 28–29). He noted the double incised lunettes across the top of the front of his chest, and that the lid was molded only on its front and back edges, features that have been found on all other members of the group. In addition, all of these pieces have bottom boards that extend at the front and sides and have a chamfered edge. This box and a closely related example (see *Portsmouth Furniture*, p. 87, *fig. 1a*) retain wooden pintle hinges. The larger chests in the group have more simplistic metal hinges. Both of the boxes exhibit elaborate decoration on the stylized three "panels" of the front. The center section on both is carved with the same heart motif and leafage, although the outer panels vary in terms of their ornament. All members of the group are of nailed-board construction. HB

3 ARMCHAIR
England, 1680–90
Beech
H. 48¼ in., S.W.14½ in., S.D. 16¼ in.
Strawbery Banke Museum; Gift of Old Colony Historical Society (1992.17)

This English cane chair has a long history of ownership in the Piscataqua region—and has an engraved silver plaque, complete with coat of arms, to prove it. As with many other "interesting relics," its condition has been compromised, and the age of the chair itself has also been questioned. Nevertheless, it has a plausible history, starting (as with so many Portsmouth "stories") in the "rambles" of the newspaperman Charles Brewster. In 1859, Brewster noted that this chair was a "handsome chair of the Elizabethan age," one of two surviving examples, he believed, that had been brought to New Hampshire in 1631 by Renald Fernald (1605–1656) and were still owned by his descendants. Fernald was a navy surgeon, and was one of about eighty emigrants who were part of Col. John Mason's Company, the initial settlers of the Portsmouth area. He signed the petition of 1653 to Massachusetts asking that the name "Strawbery Banke" be changed to the more dignified "Portsmouth." He lived on what is now known as Peirce Island and is thought to have been buried at the Point of Graves.

The chair, however, was probably made several decades after 1631, and might have been imported by one of his seven children, possibly his son Thomas (ca. 1633–1697), who lived on the islands that would become the Portsmouth Naval Shipyard and was a shipbuilder. The second chair mentioned by Brewster may be documented in a sketch (Historic New England) dated 1880 of a side chair. An accompanying note relates the Fernald family history and also states that the chair, part of a set, was given as a wedding present in 1848.

One of the principal embellishments on this chair is the carved peacock on the center of its crest rail. The same motif is also found on a daybed (Strawbery Banke Museum, 74.2) with a venerable history in the Goodwin family.

This armchair eventually was given to the Old Colony Historical Society in Taunton, Massachusetts, by Miss Louise S. Stavers (d. 1951), a native of Portsmouth and a Fernald descendant. The Society generously gave the chair to Strawbery Banke Museum in 1992, bringing it back to its original home.

4 TURNED GREAT CHAIR
Probably Boston or Charlestown,
ca. 1650–85
Probably a poplar (*Populus* spp.), ash
H. 45½ in., W. 26¾ in., D. 17⅞ in., D.
with rockers 29½ in.
Private collection

This grand turned chair, probably made in Boston or Charlestown, has been recently "discovered" and is in all likelihood one of the earliest surviving pieces of furniture with a continuous history in the greater Seacoast area. According to the research of Connie Hellwig, Bob Barth, and Hollis Brodrick, this monumental armchair was probably owned originally by one Robert Burnham (1615–1691). It remained in his family, remarkably, until 2015. Burnham arrived in New England from Norwich, England, in 1635 and initially settled in Ipswich (1635–45) and later in Boston (1645–55). By 1655, Burnham, a carpenter by trade, had moved to the Oyster River Plantation (now known as Durham) where he built a garrison house on a hill there. Burnham purchased two hundred acres of land in Oyster River from Henry Sherburne of nearby Portsmouth in 1657; that land, like this chair, did not leave the family until the twentieth century. The chair has survived in good condition, with only the loss of its handholds and the addition of rockers. Its bold posts capped with robust finials and its authoritative stance are good reminders of the hierarchical importance of armchairs in the seventeenth century. HB

5 ARMCHAIR
Portsmouth area, 1705–20
Maple, ash
H. 46 in., W. 22 in., D. 17 in.
Private collection

This early armchair is part of a group found in substantial numbers in the Seacoast area including at least two examples with a local provenance: one with a history in the Batchelder family of Hampton and another from the Wiggins family of Dover. These early chairs reflect many features of their bolder and earlier urban counterparts produced in Boston and elsewhere *(see cat. no. 4),* including the same design formula. The slightly thinner elements of this chair mark it as a member of the next generation.

Here, the three flat back slats are straight across the top at their center, and angle downward at the sides; the same shape is used for the arm blades in the horizontal plane. There are ball handholds at the top of the front posts, as well as a matched pair of cut-in round turnings on each of the front and back posts. The finials also follow a standard formula of a squat baluster with a flaring top surmounted by a large egg-shaped terminus. HB

6 CUPBOARD
Hampton, New Hampshire, area, 1710–40
Pine, probably ash
H. 59¼ in., W. 37⅛ in., D. 18¼ in.
Private collection

One of only a handful of related examples to survive from the Seacoast area, this pine cupboard of nailed board construction echoes a seventeenth-century joined form that had been popular one or two generations before it was made. The early features of this piece include the recessed upper section, with its compartments housed under the projecting roof supported at each side by turned "pillars" or columns, rendered here as thin elements reminiscent of chair stretchers. The lower section contains a tier of three drawers for storage. The sides of the case have simply been cut to form a double-arched shape that serves as the object's feet.

As with the other examples in this group of furniture—which includes chests and chests with drawers, as well as the cupboards—this cupboard represents a vernacular tradition. The cupboards provided storage space and an area for display on their tops of a family's treasured possessions of glass, ceramics, metalwares, and occasionally silver. Other examples in the group of cupboards are in the collection of the Museum of Fine Arts, Boston (32.250), and the Yale University Art Gallery (1930.2189), as well as in private collections. The fancifully painted Yale example is a key to the whole group: it was probably made for Sarah Rowell of nearby Salisbury, Massachusetts.

7 CUPBOARD
Seacoast area, probably Kittery, Maine,
1730–45
Eastern white pine
H. 76½ in., W. 33 in., D. 19½ in.
Private collection

This utilitarian pine cupboard, which retains its original red paint under an old coat of light gray, descended in the Frost family of Kittery, Maine, until the 1970s. The then-owner (still a Frost) was a direct descendant of Charles Frost (1701–1751) who married Sarah Pepperrell (1708–1797) in 1723 in Kittery. This couple was possibly the original owners of the cupboard.

The design of this vernacular cupboard—with its complex architectonic cornice, the arrangement of two paneled doors, and a large bead ornamenting the front corners of the case from top to bottom—was a standard formula in the area for much of the eighteenth century. Enough specimens have survived to indicate a pattern of popularity in a radius of about twenty-five miles around Portsmouth. This example has its original foliated H-hinges, turned wooden pulls, and ogee cutout on its base; the two doors open to reveal fixed interior shelves. It is among the most intact early examples in the group to survive. HB

8 LOOKING GLASS
Seacoast area or England, 1705–25
Possibly beech, white pine
H. 27 in., W. 13 in.
Private collection

This stately looking glass has a decorative crest (some nine inches high) with a scalloped edge and pierced openings, and also has an oval boss (or wooden ornament) applied at its center in a manner reminiscent of the seventeenth century. The crest is made of a single thin piece of veneered pine; over time, the shrinkage of the substrate has caused the crest to curl backward. The cushion-molded frame consists of an outer hardwood layer joined to a pine backing with wedges. The whole looking glass is decorated with a black-and-red tortoiseshell painted graining, applied in a distinctive angular pattern that gives the surface a great deal of life and visual appeal.

The origin of looking glasses used in early America can be difficult to determine, since many examples were imported. This example lacks an early history, although it was collected in the early twentieth century by Mrs. DeWitt Clinton (Katharine B.) Howe (later Mrs. Austin Palmer) of Hopkinton, New Hampshire. She gave it to the Currier Museum of Art (1932.1.98) in Manchester, New Hampshire, who later deaccessioned it.

A closely related mirror has surfaced recently that shares the same construction and type of graining, although it has lost its crest. This newly found looking glass (also in the same private collection) has a long history in the Goss family of Rye, New Hampshire. In the seventeenth century, they lived in the Sandy Beach area of New Castle which broke away in 1726 to become Rye. That provenance helps link both mirrors to the Seacoast area, although more work, including the microanalysis of the woods used in their construction, needs to be done in order to determine on which side of the Atlantic they were made. In either eventuality, they remain important examples of a type of furniture that was still somewhat rare in the early eighteenth century in the greater Piscataqua region. HB

9 BANISTER-BACK ARMCHAIR WITH CARVED CREST
Possibly Portsmouth, 1725–35
Maple, ash
H. 45 in., W. 25 in., D. 17 in.
Private collection

Banister-back chairs of this general type were a common form in the early baroque (or William and Mary) period in American furniture. Tall, stately, and with elegant turnings and robustly carved details, they were a staple of chair production throughout New England. This distinctive variant has been attributed to northeastern coastal Massachusetts and, as we are suggesting here, to Portsmouth. Its carving is related to that on a group of chairs, including a pair of side chairs in the Metropolitan Museum of Art and at least six other examples in private collections. The carved scrolls and foliage on the crest rails of these chairs bear markedly similar characteristics to carving on at least two other pieces of Portsmouth furniture: an altar table (St. John's Church) and a dressing table (private collection), both attributed to the cabinetmaker Joseph Davis (w. 1726–62).

The maple crest rail of this chair, as yet the only known armchair in this group, is masterfully carved and displays evidence at the back of having been riven. The crest here displays a high degree of development—it is surmounted by a foliage-carved broken scroll pediment, while the side chairs have a large C-scroll at the top. Each member of the group, however, has identical notching on all the large scrolls. They all also display leafage at the center, with opposing outward-curling leaves on each side of a central drop, and all are adorned with carved veining. This formula is also seen on the aforementioned altar table and dressing table. In addition, these chairs have double-ball turned side stretchers, a vernacular feature now generally also accepted as part of the design of more formal chairs produced in this area. The result is a tribute to the elegance that defined Portsmouth's English-based aesthetic since the beginning of the eighteenth century. HB

**10 BANISTER-BACK ARMCHAIR
WITH CARVED CREST**
Portsmouth, 1730–50
Maple, ash
H. 46¼ in., S.H. 17, W. 22½ in., S.D. 16½ in.
Private collection

The maker of this armchair made a noble effort toward producing a formal chair without abandoning the identifiable, locally familiar turnings and arms seen on much more humble straight-back examples. The finials, back posts, and underarm turnings are all familiar features on everyday examples from the Seacoast area. The finials, with their down-turned central knop, and the simplistic turning of the lower part of the stiles, as well as the under-arm turnings, parrot features more commonly seen on much simpler straight-back models. The sawn-out arms, with their characteristic "dropped" handholds, have long been recognized as a detail characteristic of chairs from this region and are seen on dozens of examples.

At least three side chairs by this same maker have been identified, all of which exhibit the same turned and split banisters which are of a different profile than the side stiles, a detail which varies from the norm. The finely carved crest rail seen here, also common to this group, almost seems out of place on an otherwise vernacular chair. Crests by this same carver have also been found on chairs by two other distinctively different turner-chairmakers who were more well-versed in the prototypes provided by more formal Boston seating. HB

**11A BANISTER-BACK SIDE CHAIR
WITH FISH-TAIL CREST**
Portsmouth area, 1740–90
Maple
H. 43½ in., W. 19¼ in., D. 15¼ in.
Private collection

The side chair here *(cat. no. 11A)* is perhaps the stateliest example of the known fish-tail crest examples. It is the most formal rendition of this locally popular vernacular type, usually seen in more rudimentary expressions, and exhibits a well-designed formula and vigorous components not often seen in the general type. Its turnings are well articulated and boldly conceived, clearly produced by a seasoned master chairmaker. One would perhaps expect to see a carved crest rail on such a finely turned chair, but the fish-tail crest, more common on much simpler chairs, nevertheless serves as a fitting top for this elegant example.

Other features, both turned and molded, also indicate its local production. The ogee-molded stay rail, across the base of the back, shares a commonality with other turned furniture from

11B BANISTER-BACK ARMCHAIR
WITH FISH-TAIL CREST
Portsmouth area, 1740–90
Probably maple, ash
H. 42 in., W. 26 in., D. 17 in.
Private collection

11C BANISTER-BACK ARMCHAIR
WITH FISH-TAIL CREST
Portsmouth area, 1740–90
Black-painted maple, other woods
H. 46 in., W. 19¼ in., D. 13¾ in.
Collection of Craig and Alison Jewett

the area, being related to the molded stretchers on a group of splayed-base tables and to the stay rails and side stretchers on a group of chairs in the Queen Anne style with Spanish feet. The turnings on the front legs also bear similarities to related details on these tables and Queen Anne chairs. The double-ball side stretchers here can also be found on other, more formal banister-back chairs attributed to this area.

The two armchairs demonstrate other variations. The smaller chair *(cat. no. 11B)* has the standard local turnings and crest rail, but its swooping arms with rounded handholds are not typical, although at least three other identical examples are known. The larger example *(cat. no. 11C)* deviates dramatically from the norm in its turnings and in its more archaic crest, but retains the "droopy" handholds so familiar in chairs from this region. HB

12 SLAT-BACK ARMCHAIR
Portsmouth area, 1730–80
Maple, ash
H. 47¾ in., W. 23½ in., D. 20
Collection of Craig and Alison Jewett

Identifiable slat-back chairs from the Piscataqua region are uncommon today although they initially were commonplace. Although side chairs can be very difficult to regionalize, armchairs such as this offer a few more diagnostic clues that can help pinpoint their origin. This turned, four-slat example is taller than most from our region; it retains a coat of gray paint over a coat of red. It displays the "standard" so-called sausage-turned posts commonly used on chairs of this form throughout New England. However, it also features serpentine arms with drooping handholds and baluster turnings below the arms and above the seat. These details are found on literally dozens of banister-back armchairs from this area, including many with strong provenance (see *Portsmouth Furniture, cat. nos. 73, 74*). Such chairs were a common product of local chairmakers, who made them in quantity for export as well as for local use. HB

**13 SLAT-BACK ARMCHAIR
WITH DRINKING ARM**
Portsmouth area, 1735–70
Maple, ash, pine
H. 47¾ in., W. 22 in., D. 17 in.
(not including arm)
Private collection

Published in 1921 in Wallace Nutting's *Furniture of the Pilgrim Century, 1620–1720* (p. 281), when it was owned by the legendary dealer Israel Sack, this slat-back armchair exhibits many characteristics of the Seacoast area. But it also sports an unusual feature: a pine "drinking arm," affixed to the proper left arm support, which both tilts and swivels. When in the horizontal position, as illustrated here, the round surface provides a convenient place about a foot in diameter for such articles as spectacles, reading material, and a mug, cann, or tankard. Reminiscent of a writing-arm Windsor, this device offers less surface area but more flexibility, and is testimony to the New England penchant for inventive, innovative solutions. Although Nutting dates the chair to 1720–30, it probably was made a little later in the eighteenth century. Remarkably, a second example (private collection), probably by the same maker and featuring the same swivel attachment, has also survived.

14 TABLE
Portsmouth, New Castle, New Hampshire, or southern Maine, 1735–60
Maple   H. 21½ in., W. 24¼ in., D. 33½ in.
New Hampshire Historical Society; Gift of Katharine Prentis Murphy and Edmund Astley, Jr.,
in Memory of David Edward Murphy (1957.065.03.16)

This striking table is one of at least seven related examples long associated with the Piscataqua region. Some sources record that this table was found in New Castle, New Hampshire, but others have suggested that it actually was discovered across the river in Kittery, Maine (see *Portsmouth Furniture*, pp. 218–20). Regardless of its precise origin, the form is one of the most dramatic and (in the word of the furniture scholar Frances Gruber Safford) *arresting* table forms made in early America. Its boldly splayed and crisply turned legs end in Spanish feet and support a frame distinguished by an elegantly arched and shaped skirt. Many of its details are also found on a group of related chairs that may be from the same shop *(see cat. no. 18)*. The whole is capped by a wide, oval, overhanging top. The result is a dynamic table that seems possessed by energy.

15 HIGH CHEST OF DRAWERS
Portsmouth, 1733
Maple, black walnut, maple and
black walnut veneer, eastern white pine
H. 86¼ in., W. 40½ in., D. 22¼ in.
Warner House Association;
Gift of Ruth and Thaxter Brown (WH 1993.1)

When prominently featured in *Portsmouth Furniture* (see pp. 124–27, colorplate 3, and the dust jacket), this important high chest was still in a private collection. The inlaid inscription in its pediment—"I + S / 1733"—suggests that the piece was owned by John Sherburne (1706–ca. 1736), a merchant of Portsmouth, and made in 1733, which, in the words of furniture scholar Brock Jobe, make it "the earliest dated example of American furniture in the Queen Anne style" (*Portsmouth Furniture*, p. 125). Aside from its documentary significance, this high chest makes a marvelous visual statement, achieving a great deal of richness and complexity through its use of herringbone banding surrounding its veneered drawers and various inlaid details. Like all but one Portsmouth high chest of this style *(see cat. no. 17)*, this has lost its original legs; they have subsequently been replaced. Since it was given to the Warner House Association in 1993, the high chest has become a part of the collection in the magnificent house built by Archibald Macpheadris (1680–1728) on Daniel Street in 1716. It had been there since the early nineteenth century, when it was brought into the house by a later marriage.

16 HIGH CHEST OF DRAWERS
Joseph Davis (w. 1726–62)
Portsmouth, 1735–45
Black walnut, walnut veneer,
birch, eastern white pine
H. 75 in., W. 40¼ in., D. 22⅜ in.
Strawbery Banke Museum;
Gift of Mary Neale Kendall (1991.191)

This high chest, signed by Joseph Davis in chalk on one of its drawer bottoms, is a key piece in the understanding of Portsmouth furniture in the second quarter of the eighteenth century. Only one other piece, a dressing table, is known with a Davis signature (see *Portsmouth Furniture*, p. 47, *fig. 29*). Trained in Boston by Job Coit (1718–1742), Davis arrived in Portsmouth in the early 1730s. Some of his work, like this high chest, is heavily indebted to Boston-area furniture, but some of his other forms are more innovative in their details.

At some time in its life, as often happened with these case pieces, this high chest had lost all four of its legs; the front two were replaced with cabriole legs, but simple, straight posts were used to form the rear legs (see *Portsmouth Furniture*, p. 46, *fig. 28*). In 2015, a generous donor helped Strawbery Banke Museum replace all four legs with more appropriately shaped cabriole legs based on the original legs of the related high chest *(cat. no. 17)* seen here.

17 HIGH CHEST OF DRAWERS
Joseph Davis (w. 1726–62)
Portsmouth, 1735–45
Walnut, walnut veneer, eastern white pine
H. 75¼ in., W. 48¼ in., D. 25¼ in.
Private collection

An exciting new discovery, this imposing high chest of drawers joins a small group that can be attributed to Joseph Davis of Portsmouth, including the signed example at Strawbery Banke Museum in this exhibition *(cat. no. 16)*. This high chest is the only member of the group to retain its original cabriole legs terminating in pad feet. It is broad in stance and bold in execution, achieving a monumentality rarely seen in these early high chests. Enriched with a robust shell on its lower central drawer and extraordinary carved pilasters on its upper case, it is testimony to the carver's as well as the cabinetmaker's art. Carefully selected walnut veneers endow the surface with the shimmering, active optical effects that are a hallmark of the baroque aesthetic. The heavily molded, architectonic pediment here is a recent replacement, modeled after the Davis high chest in the collection of the United States Department of State collection (74.68; see also *Portsmouth Furniture, cat. no. 16)*. Another similar Davis-attributed high chest (private collection) also emerged in the last few years, with connections to the Simes and Wentworth families, adding to the record of this important Portsmouth cabinetmaker.

18 SIDE CHAIR
Portsmouth, 1735–45
Maple, ash
H. 39½ in., W. 19½ in., D. 17 in.
Private collection

This Queen Anne side chair is part of group of elegant chairs known for their unusually bold yet delicate form. The back splats of this group are more broad and delicate than is customarily seen. The front stretchers on this group come both in this unusual model and the more usual configuration of two balls with a reel between. The baluster turnings of the front legs begin with a delicately undercut cove turning at the base of each. The front legs terminate at the base with simple, flaring, three-toed Spanish feet which are one piece with the legs. Both side stretchers and the stay rail are adorned with an ogee molding. These last three mentioned features are also found on the group of local splay-legged tables *(see cat. no. 14)* which were probably made in the same shop. HB

19 SIDE CHAIR
Attributed to John Gaines III (1704–1743)
Portsmouth, 1735–40
H. 39⅞ in., W. 18¼ in., D. 19 in.
Collection of Craig and Alison Jewett

Chairmaking was a staple of Portsmouth's furniture-making industry for much of the eighteenth century. Chairs featuring the design elements seen in this example—the distinctive carved crest rail, vase-shaped splat, shaped skirt, ball-and-ring front stretcher, and turned legs ending in Spanish feet—are associated with John Gaines III, a craftsman trained by his father in Ipswich, Massachusetts, and active in Portsmouth in the second quarter of the century. Key specimens in this attribution are chairs at Strawbery Banke Museum (1998.125) with a history in the Gaines/Brewster family. This chair was from the collection of the famed collector Mitchell M. Taradash (1889–1973).

Like many objects misnamed "transitional" by some authors or termed "compromise solutions" by others, chairs such as this exhibit characteristics of more than one of the international styles popular in the period. From the waist down, it could well be from the William and Mary period, while from the seat up it makes a nod to the Queen Anne aesthetic in its solid splat and yoke-shaped crest rail, while still retaining a carved crest that is almost an abstracted echo of the more elaborate carving found on earlier chairs. Such idiosyncratic combinations are popular in many provincial and rural areas.

20 SIDE CHAIR
Probably Portsmouth, 1735–75
Maple
H. 41⅞ in., W. 20¼ in., D. 17 in.
Collection of Craig and Alison Jewett

This elegant Queen Anne side chair has an unusually shaped splat, a design probably derived from English examples dating earlier in the eighteenth century. Other chairs with this distinctive splat and embellished with carved crest rails, and presumably from the same shop, have surfaced in this area for years, several of which have histories of ownership in nearby towns. An armchair in the collection of the Currier Museum of Art (1963.20) is probably by the same craftsman who fashioned this chair: it shares an identical crest rail, splat, and front and side skirt cut-outs. It has a history of having been owned by Josiah Bartlett (1729–1795) of Kingston, New Hampshire, one of the state's three signers of the Declaration of Independence.

Three earlier Queen Anne chairs which are also very English in feeling and date to about 1735–45 have also survived with histories in the Portsmouth area—one of them descended in the Jaffrey family. Although they vary in many ways, including having cabriole legs, they feature the same splat and have extremely similar seat-frame cut-outs.

This beautiful example is somewhat unusual in that it has Spanish feet; most examples have turned ones. It also retains a striking surface treatment of red-and-black painted graining with gilt striping that may date to the early nineteenth century. HB

21 LOW CHAIR
Portsmouth, 1730–60
Probably maple
H. 39½ in., W. 20 in, D. 15 in.
Private collection

In the eighteenth century, a chair with a lower seat height, such as this Portsmouth-area example, was usually called in documents a "low chair." Generally known today to collectors as a "slipper chair," it is likely that their reduced seat height provided a convenient platform for dressing in bedchambers (and putting on shoes). While they were often made on special order as single items, on occasion, as with a Massachusetts set at the Museum of Fine Arts, Boston, a low chair (1972.123) was made en suite with a set of regular-sized examples. They were popular during the period of the Queen Anne and Chippendale styles.

This chair possesses an earmark feature that helps determine its origin: its simple, abstracted, molded crest rail. This unusual yoke shape lacks the usual "kick-up" shaping at the inner points of each of the two arches. And, unlike almost all New England chairs of this type, the crest lacks the usual volutes at the inner base of its two arches. Four other full-size chairs of this type, by at least three different makers, have been discovered locally. All share the same type of crest rail. HB

22 MARBLE SLAB TABLE
Possibly by Timothy Davis III (ca. 1715–1772) or Joseph Buss Jr. (d. 1762)
Probably Portsmouth, 1730–60
Walnut
H. 32⅞ in., W. 56 in., D. 20½ in.
Portsmouth Athenaeum

Thought to have been owned originally by Sir William Pepperrell (1696–1759), this grand table originally had a marble top (or slab), now replaced with a grained wooden substitute. It is related stylistically to a larger table in the Winterthur Museum collection (1965.3093), once attributed to Timothy Davis III (ca. 1715–1772) of Portsmouth and Berwick, Maine, and probably owned originally by a John Hill (1703–1772) of Berwick. However, in more recent years the Winterthur table has been re-attributed to Portsmouth and assigned to Davis or his uncle, Joseph Buss, Jr., although other fine cabinetmakers capable of producing work at this level were active here as well. As a high-style and initially very expensive walnut example in the Queen Anne mode, the Pepperrell table stands in stark contrast to "Molly's" vernacular table of maple and of about the same date *(cat. no. 23)*, given, according to tradition, by Sir William to his enslaved person, Molly Miles.

In the nineteenth century, this table wound up at the Wentworth-Coolidge mansion in Little Harbor before finding its way to the Athenaeum. The rear rail has been cut to accommodate a chair rail and thus it was probably used against the wall, like most but not all examples.

23 TABLE ("MOLLY'S TABLE")
Seacoast area, ca. 1750 with later alterations
Maple; two replaced legs, oak
H. 27 in., Diam. 27 in.
Portsmouth Historical Society; Gift of Alan and Anne Cutter (2017.2)

A nineteenth-century pencil inscription on the underside of this table's top elevates it from a ordinary object in poor condition to a document of great interest in the history of the Seacoast area. As the notation records: "This table came from / Sir William Pepperell. / He gave it to his slave / Molly Miles." Research by Patricia Q. Wall, presented in her forthcoming book *Lives of Consequence*, has identified Molly Miles (ca. 1718–1827) as an enslaved person owned by Sir William Pepperrell (1696–1759) of Kittery Point and later members of his family. New England eighteenth-century objects with a history of ownership by an enslaved person are exceedingly rare.

Although details of her life are scant, Molly's death in the Eliot almshouse was recorded in the *Portsmouth Journal of Literature & Politics*. The notice recorded her age of nearly 108 years, and noted that "she retained the faculties of her mind to the last, walking perfectly erect, with a firm step, and had not a wrinkle on her face, and could distinctly see to read her Bible without glasses; she walked to Kittery Point a year ago last summer, a distance of twelve miles in one day, and then did not complain much of fatigue."

The table's top has been reduced by about six inches in diameter (according to another inscription) and two of the original legs have been replaced with oak substitutes. At some time, the table entered into the Foye family. Research by the donor, the Reverend Alan Cutter, has traced it through several generations, including a stint when it served as a television stand.

24A ARMCHAIR
Attributed to Robert Harrold (w. 1765–92)
Portsmouth, 1765–75
Mahogany
H. 37½ in., W. 28 in., D. 18½ in.
Private collection

This armchair *(cat. no. 24A)* features elements that link it to a large body of related examples attributed to the shop of Robert Harrold, the English immigrant who had such a profound impact on Portsmouth furniture in the rococo or Chippendale style (see *Portsmouth Furniture, cat. no. 86).* Its splat design is based on a plate in Robert Manwaring's pattern book entitled *The Cabinet and Chair-Maker's Real Friend and Companion* (1765), a demonstration of the increasing importance of design books in the second half of the eighteenth century.

One side chair here *(cat. no. 24B)*, also in the rococo style, is probably from a different shop. More than sixty examples of this general type, featuring slight variations on the splat design, have been linked to Portsmouth (see *Portsmouth Furniture, cat. no. 88).* The second side chair *(cat. no. 24C)* presents some interesting possibilities. It was sold at auction in 2014 with a history in a Skowhegan, Maine, family said to have roots in Portsmouth. Made of dense mahogany and with an English-style seat construction featuring front corner braces rather than glue blocks, the chair features a ribbon-back design that was popular in England and various parts of America, including several variants associated with Portsmouth (see *Portsmouth Furniture, cat. no. 90).* In recent years, other chairs of this type have been attributed to the English-trained Harrold.

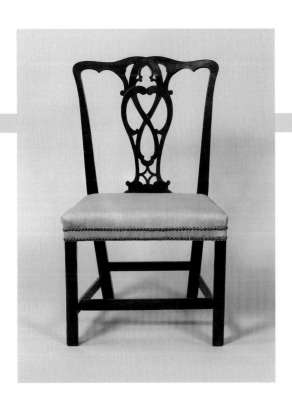

24B SIDE CHAIR
Portsmouth, 1765–75
Mahogany
H. 37¾ in., W. 22 in., D. 18½ in.
Moffatt–Ladd House & Garden

24C SIDE CHAIR
Possibly Portsmouth or England, 1765–75
Mahogany, possibly beech or maple
H. 38 in., W. 22⅛ in., D. 20½ in.
Douglas Nelson and Karin Cullity Nelson

25 KETTLE STAND
Attributed to Robert Harrold (w. 1765–92)
Portsmouth, 1765–75
Mahogany, white pine, cherry
H. 26⅛ in., W. 12⅞ in., D. 12¾ in.
Moffatt-Ladd House & Garden;
Gift of Robert J. Mead (2009.4)

Only two examples of this Portsmouth type of kettle stand are known: this one, given to the Moffatt-Ladd House by a family descendant in 2009; and another, now at the Warner House, that descended in the Wendell family. Another similar stand, not yet examined, remains in a private collection and may become the third such table to have survived. Along with a small group of closely related china (or tea) tables—and an eighth example of this select group was just discovered—they speak to the best aspects of high-style Portsmouth furniture in the rococo mode (see *Portsmouth Furniture, cat. nos. 49, 50*).

Robert Harrold, a London-trained immigrant, probably made this stand, and he packed a lot of his knowledge and background into its design and fabrication. The kettle stand is notable for its straight so-called Marlborough-legs ending in squared feet, and for its graceful arched stretchers culminating in a distinctive pierced finial. Designed to hold a silver tea kettle or urn, the stand is also fitted with a slide to hold a single cup. It formed an important part of the constellation of objects that facilitated the tea-drinking ritual that was such an important part of social life in the eighteenth century. This elegant object reinforces the predominant English influence evident in Portsmouth and other parts of colonial America on the cusp of the American Revolution.

26 DESK
Portsmouth, 1800–1810
Mahogany, bird's-eye maple veneer, pine
H. 35 in., W. 29⅝ in., D. 17¾ in.
Moffatt-Ladd House & Garden; Gift of Emily Sullivan Laighton Holman (1994.2)

This small writing desk is part of a group of related examples linked to Portsmouth, although the form was made elsewhere in New England as well (see *Portsmouth Furniture, cat. no. 29*). Here, a hinged upper section unfolds to form a sloped writing surface and reveal small compartments for writing implements. A single drawer, extending the full width of the case here, provides additional storage space. This example is notable for its striking bird's-eye maple veneer that gives its surface such a wonderful variegated and bright appearance.

27 DRESSING TABLE OR SERVER
Portsmouth, 1800–1810
Mahogany, mahogany veneer, light-wood inlays, pine
H. 36¾ in., W. 41½ in., D. 22½ in.
Moffatt-Ladd House & Garden; Gift of Isabel Marvin King (Mrs. Archer E. King, Jr.) (1993.4)

Small dressing tables or servers such as this example are an unusual form closely associated with the Portsmouth area (see *Portsmouth Furniture, cat. no. 21*). Other examples are in the collection of Historic New England, the Portsmouth Historical Society, and in various other public and private collections. This example, probably by Judkins and Senter or Langley Boardman, was said to have been in Boardman's home on Middle Street when it was acquired by the donor's father, William Marvin, in 1900. Notable for its slender legs and carefully selected veneers, the table represents Portsmouth's finest work in the federal period.

28 SIDEBOARD
Attributed to Judkins and Senter (w. 1808–26), Portsmouth, ca. 1815
Mahogany, mahogany veneer, flame birch veneer, pine
H. 42½ in., W. 71 in., D. 24 in.
Moffatt-Ladd House & Garden; Museum purchase (2014.001)

This is one of a small handful of neoclassical sideboards, including examples at Strawbery Banke Museum and the New Hampshire Historical Society, that can be attributed with a great deal of certainty to the prominent Portsmouth cabinetmaking partnership of Jonathan Judkins (1780–1844) and William Senter (1783–1827). The Wendell family sideboard at Strawbery Banke is dated 1815, providing a good approximate date for this closely related example. It is embellished with similarly colorful and contrasting veneers of dark mahogany and light flame birch. In excellent condition, this sideboard, unfortunately, lacks an early history.

In the federal period, it became more common to set aside a specific room for dining in wealthy homes. Sideboards, a new form in that era, formed an essential component of those spaces, sometimes placed within an arched, recessed niche created especially for them. They were designed to hold and display ceramic, glass, and silver tablewares, textiles, wine bottles, knife (or cutlery) boxes, and other accoutrements associated with dining, including (on occasion) a chamber pot for the use of gentlemen after the ladies had withdrawn.

29A CARD TABLE
Portsmouth, 1790–1810
Mahogany, mahogany
veneer, possibly birch
inlay, pine
H. 28½ in., W. 35¼ in.,
D. closed 17¾ in.
Private collection

This card table *(cat. 29A)*, branded "W. RICE," is one of a small group of objects thought to have been owned originally by William Rice (1767–1851), including a chair and a sea chest (see *Portsmouth Furniture*, p. 435) and a sideboard (private collection). Rice was a wealthy merchant and privateer who lived on Deer Street and died possessed of a substantial estate. His house, an earlier mansion he acquired in 1804, survives, having been moved to 408 The Hill.

Often made in pairs, card tables provided a venue for card playing and, on occasion, high-stakes gambling. This example is in a common shape—square with ovolo corners—used for more than 25 percent of all American federal-period card tables, according to the research of Benjamin A. Hewitt. Its inlaid patera closely match those found on the Pembroke table seen here *(cat. no. 29B)*. Branded "PURCELL," this table is one of the few objects associated with the family that built what is now called the John Paul Jones house. This table was probably owned by Nancy (1767–1843) or Susan Purcell (ca. 1777–1861), daughters of Gregory (d. 1776) and Sarah Purcell (d.1783), who had built the house in about 1758 (see *Portsmouth Furniture, cat. no. 57*).

The elegant tiger-maple dressing table here *(cat. no. 29C)*, part of a group of related Portsmouth examples (see *Portsmouth Furniture, cat. no. 23*), has a history in the prominent Thaxter family of the Seacoast area.

29B PEMBROKE TABLE
Portsmouth, 1795–1810
Mahogany, mahogany veneer, birch inlay, soft maple, eastern white pine
H. 27$^9/_{16}$ in., W. 33$^7/_8$ in., D. closed 20$^1/_8$ in.
Private collection; on loan to the Portsmouth Historical Society

29C DRESSING TABLE
Portsmouth, 1805–1820
Tiger maple, ebony and light- and dark-wood inlay, pine
H. 39 in., W. 36 in., D. 17$^1/_4$ in.
Michael and Gloria Reopel

30A SIDE CHAIR
Probably Portsmouth, 1805–15
Painted maple, sweet gum, cherry
H. 34⅞ in., W. 18½ in., D. 19 in.
New Hampshire Historical Society;
Purchase with funds provided by
Mr. and Mrs. James L. Garvin (2014.012)

30B CHEST OF DRAWERS
Portsmouth, 1810–20
Mahogany, mahogany veneer, birch veneer, pine
H. 37½ in., W. 43¾ in., D. 21½ in.
New Hampshire Historical Society;
Purchase with funds provided by
Mr. and Mrs. James L. Garvin (2014.011)

Each of these federal-period pieces bears the brand of Lewis Barnes (1776–1856), their original owner. Barnes, a Swedish immigrant, was a merchant and a sea captain. As befitting a member of the Federal Fire Society, Barnes apparently took seriously the concept of branding his furniture so that it could be identified and claimed after a potential fire. At least sixteen

pieces have survived stamped with his name (see *Portsmouth Furniture*, p. 426), as well as at least one of his fire buckets. Barnes used his furniture in his house on Islington Street, fragments of which still survive incorporated into a gas station.

The chair *(cat. no. 30A)* was once part of a large set of eight chairs and two settees that has been dispersed and is now scattered in several public and private collections. Such fancy-painted chairs were made in Portsmouth, but were also imported from New York and elsewhere, and determining their place of manufacture can be difficult *(see cat. no. 31)*. The elliptic-front chest of drawers *(cat. no. 30B)* features many details that link it to high-quality federal-period Portsmouth furniture, including the form of its corner posts, its leg turnings, and the use of a light-colored "wavy" birch veneer that plays off the darker mahogany veneer to create the dynamic color contrasts that are an essential part of the aesthetic of northern New England furniture in this period.

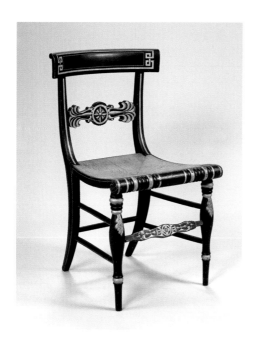

31 SIDE CHAIR
New York, New England,
or possibly Portsmouth, 1815–30
Painted wood, rush seat
H. 33 in., W. 19¼ in., D. 16¼ in.
Portsmouth Historical Society;
Gift of Edith Harris (1)

"Fancy painted" chairs of this type were a popular component of the chairmaker's craft during the late classical period. Evoking the ancient klismos form, this chair, part of a set of at least five, is painted black with gilt trim and classical details. Although an attractive treatment, much of this decoration was probably applied or renewed in the late nineteenth century and covers a red ocher ground that may have been part of the original surface.

Such chairs were made in Portsmouth in the early nineteenth century but were also imported in large quantities; the origin of this chair is thus difficult to pinpoint with accuracy. A large set of painted seating furniture, for example, was purchased by the Wendell family of Portsmouth from a New York firm (now at Strawbery Banke Museum); a set with a Warner House history was probably imported from Boston or Philadelphia.

Edith Kimball Harris (1868–1956), the donor of this chair, may have inherited it from her family. Born in California, Harris was a world traveler who eventually settled in Portsmouth, living with her sister Mary in their house at 43 Austin Street for many years. She was a member of the Society of Arts and Crafts, Boston, as a metalworker, although no example of her work in that vein is known to the writer. Some of her correspondence and works on paper, as well as many photographs of her, are in the collection of the Portsmouth Athenaeum.

32 WORKTABLE
New England, possibly Portsmouth, 1815–25
Mahogany, mahogany veneer, white pine
H. 28½ in., W. closed 19½ in., D. 18 in.
Portsmouth Historical Society;
Gift of Ann L. Shackford (476)

Furniture can possess different meanings for different audiences. For a furniture collector, this table presents some issues: its front legs have been damaged and re-attached; one of its interior drawers has been reduced in size; and its finish has degraded over time. Its manufacture in New England seems secure, but it may have been made in Boston, Salem, or Portsmouth. Social historians, however, are more interested in the role small tables like this played in the daily activities of women in the early nineteenth century, as it provided surfaces and storage spaces, including the cloth bag (replaced here) below the two small drawers, all helpful features for sewing and writing.

Local historians and genealogists also find value in this table because it has a history of ownership by Anne Eustis Langdon (1771–1818), the wife of Henry Sherburne Langdon (1776–1858). These Langdons lived in the John Paul Jones house in the early nineteenth century, and this table is thus one of the very few objects that has an early association with the house. Since Anne Eustis Langdon died in 1818, however, it is possible that this table was not used originally by her, but by one of her two daughters, Ann or Elizabeth. Pushing back the history of ownership of an object by a generation is not an uncommon practice.

33 CHILD'S CHAIR
New England, possibly Portsmouth, 1825–50
Painted wood, replaced upholstery
H. 26 in., W. 14¼ in., D. 12½ in.
Portsmouth Historical Society; Gift of Mrs. James H. Dow (720)

Typical of many such factory chairs made in the second quarter of the nineteenth century, and later, this small child's chair is notable for its gold stenciled decoration of a lyre and foliage on its crest rail and basket of fruit and other motifs on its vase-shaped splat. The seat, originally caned, has been fitted with a late nineteenth-century textile show cover featuring floral designs in shades of brown outlined by a wavy brown gimp that is tacked in place. Such an adaptation suggests that this charming child's chair might have been a valued family heirloom worthy of preservation for the enjoyment of several generations. It came to the Society as part of a large number of objects from the Dow family.

34 WASHSTAND
New England, possibly Portsmouth, 1830–50
Mahogany, mahogany veneer, pine
H. 37 in., W. 20¾ in., D. 15¾ in.
Portsmouth Historical Society; Gift of Lawrence B. Craig (735)

In a form evocative of daily life before indoor plumbing and running water, this mahogany washstand of the mid nineteenth century provides an open space, nine inches in diameter, on its top shelf for a small water basin for washing or shaving. This is flanked by two smaller cut-outs for soap holders or other accoutrements. The lower shelf provides space for a pitcher, larger basin, or chamber pot. With well-turned legs and a dramatic scroll serving as a small splashboard, this well-made washstand features a mahogany backboard and drawer linings. It is a well-made and fashionable example that has been in the collection of the Portsmouth Historical Society for many years and might well have been made here.

35 CHEST OF DRAWERS
Samuel Dockum (1792–1872)
Portsmouth, 1835–50
Mahogany, mahogany veneer, pine
H. 51⅛ in., W. 45 in., D. 22½ in.
Portsmouth Historical Society;
Gift of Serena Jones (238)

This large chest of drawers, along with several other pieces, came to the Portsmouth Historical Society from Serena Jones with a history of having been made by her ancestor, Samuel Dockum, one of Portsmouth's most prominent nineteenth-century furniture makers. Like many other objects of its time, its design echoes the forms, heavy moldings, and large scrolls pictured in John Hall's *Cabinet Maker's Assistant: Embracing the Most Modern Style of Cabinet Furniture* (Baltimore: John Murphy, 1840). Hall shows related dressing bureaus, for example, as his figures 171 and 173, which vary in some details but which share the scrolled feet, broad proportions, and wide drawers flanked by scrolls seen here. Hall's pattern book, however, captured a plain, Grecian style that had already been popular throughout the United States for about a decade, and this Dockum piece could have been made in the 1830s or the 1840s. In the absence of carving, inlay, or other decorative details, it relies for its visual success solely on its massing and well-selected, thinly cut mahogany veneers.

36 DESK
Samuel Passmore Treadwell (1816–1906)
Portsmouth, 1858
Mahogany, mahogany veneer, rosewood
veneer, cherry, eastern white pine
H. 49¼ in., W. 38 in., D. 26 in.
Portsmouth Historical Society;
Gift of Winona and Michael Reid in
Memory of Gilman Abar (2015.006)

A pencil inscription on the underside of the hinged writing surface of this unusual desk provides the name of its maker and its date of manufacture: "S.P. Treadwell / Portsmouth N.H. / Made 1858." Samuel Passmore Treadwell was a long-lived native of Portsmouth who began his cabinetmaking career with the Brown and Joy firm on Market Street. After several moves, he returned to Portsmouth in 1849 where he was elected to the first city council. He later served as an alderman, collector of taxes, and for many years as city treasurer. A staunch Democrat, he also was elected to the New Hampshire House for a term and worked as the election moderator in Ward 1. He lived at 13 Ladd Street.

His desk, presumably made for his own use, descended in the family to the donor, the great-great-granddaughter of the maker. It has a sloped writing surface at center, and also features two vertical box-like compartments at each side of the rear, each divided internally into tiers of small pigeon-holes. The lower section is embellished with brass stringing, and the elegant turned legs with brass collars are detachable. No other furniture by Treadwell is known to the writer.

37A MINIATURE TABLE
Attributed to Edmund M. Brown (1803–1883)
Portsmouth, ca. 1850
Mahogany
H. 5 ¾ in., Diam. 6⅝ in.
Warner House Association; Gift of Andrew H. Brown (WH1953.9)

37B MINIATURE SOFA
Attributed to Edmund M. Brown (1803–1883)
Portsmouth, ca. 1848
Mahogany
H. 5 ¾ in, W. 13 ¾ in., D. 4 ½ in.
Warner House Association; Gift of Andrew H. Brown (WH1953.8)

Some inscriptions and their Brown family history suggest that these charming miniature objects might have been made in the mid nineteenth century by Edmund M. Brown, a Portsmouth cabinetmaker. The sofa, which retains its original upholstery showing evidence of much use, is inscribed in black ink under the seat with the name "Brown," preceded by illegible initials, the date "April 24, 1848," and the notation "No. 1." It also bears a later pencil notation reading: "For [illegible] / From Ella June 10, 1907." The center table lacks inscriptions.

Other works attributed to Edmund M. Brown include a cane (671) and a portable writing desk (750) in the collection of the Portsmouth Historical Society. During his long career he was a partner at various times with Samuel Dockum and Samuel P. Treadwell, cabinetmakers who are also represented in this exhibition.

38 MARBLE-TOP TABLE
Samuel Dockum (1792–1872)
Portsmouth, 1860–70
Mahogany, marble
H. 37 in., W. 16 in., D. 12⅛ in.
Portsmouth Historical Society; Gift of Serena Jones (2013.069)

This small marble-topped stand or table, perhaps used in a hallway, is typical of the furnishings that cluttered many interiors in the mid nineteenth century. The ornament here, including the castellated band of ornament on each side of the top of the frame, the incised lines and ring turnings of the shaft and center passage of the piece, and the roundels at the top of the four curved legs, enriched with stamped clover-leaf designs, all point to the types of decoration popular in the third quarter of the century and later. The table came to the Portsmouth Historical Society with a history of having been made by Samuel Dockum, who died in 1872. If the family tradition is accurate, this table is probably one of the last works from his shop.

39 CHEST
Hampton, New Hampshire, area, ca. 1758
Eastern white pine
H. 17 in., W. 53 ½ in., D. 19 in.
Private collection

This capacious six-board chest is a rare and early example of a colonial American military "foot locker" used in the French and Indian War; most surviving chests date from the Revolutionary era. These utilitarian chests usually follow the same rugged construction formula, featuring nailed board construction. It also has iron reinforcing braces nailed in place on the corners and iron hinges securing the lid. The officer's name is usually emblazoned across the top of the lid, and they often have carrying handles on the ends to facilitate handling and hauling when transported by wagon. A till on the inside provided space for small and valuable articles that might otherwise be hard to find in the cavernous chest.

Here, the inscription "Capt. Jon^a Swett New Hampshire 1758" with a decorative tendril and berry scroll at the end is scratch carved across nearly the full width of the lid. Capt. Jonathan Swett (1712–ca. 1768) was from Hampton Falls, New Hampshire. In 1758, New Hampshire raised a regiment of eight hundred men commanded by Col. John Hart of Portsmouth. Part of the regiment formed an expedition against the fortress of Louisburg while the remainder were sent to guard the western frontier of New Hampshire against possible French incursions. Capt. Swett's company was stationed there at Fort Westmoreland, or Fort No. 2 in the line of western forts, in the town of that name. HB

40 TOOL CHEST
Probably Portsmouth, ca. 1800
Pine, iron handles
H. 30 in., W. 29¼ in., D. 17¼ in.
Portsmouth Historical Society; Gift of Hollis Brodrick (2017.1)

Utilitarian furniture forms such as this craftsman's tool chest are rare survivals. Made to be used daily, they lack the stylistic embellishments that often lead to the preservation of old furniture. This chest was probably owned by William Cadogan Simes (1773–1824), a Portsmouth silversmith active from 1795 until his death. The drawer blade under the top drawer is branded "W. SIMES" in the manner many Portsmouth citizens used to identify their furniture; this previously unidentified brand has not been found on any other Portsmouth objects. The low chest is of dovetailed construction, never had feet, and has iron pulls on its drawers. Each drawer was once fitted for a lock, and the chest also has iron carrying handles on its side, suggesting that Simes may have used it occasionally as a traveling chest. The inventories of silversmith's shops indicate that utilitarian chests or "cases" of drawers were often used to store the many tools and supplies necessary to operate even a small shop in the eighteenth and early nineteenth centuries.

Simes, trained by his brother-in-law Martin Parry (1758–1802), took over his relative's shop in 1795 when he reached his majority. As was typical of most Portsmouth silversmiths, he principally made various forms of flatware (including several examples in the collection of the Portsmouth Historical Society), retailed objects, and did repair work. The most notable surviving objects attributed to him are a pair of water pitchers made in 1817 for the Cilley family, but he seems to have largely been what was known as a "smallworker" in the parlance of the day.

41 BATHTUB
Probably Portsmouth, 1780–1820
Mahogany
H. 17½ in., W. approx. 24 in., L. 75½ in.
Portsmouth Historical Society; lent by the Hon. Woodbury Langdon, July 1, 1920 (651)

This extraordinary bathtub was one of the curious articles exhibited at the John Paul Jones (JPJ) house when it opened as a museum in 1920. Its lender, the Hon. Woodbury Langdon (1836–1921), also supplied the funds that enabled the acquisition of the house by the newly formed Portsmouth Historical Society. The bathtub may have had a history in his family, although its early history is unknown.

The bathtub consists of a single, hollowed-out piece of mahogany, resembling a dugout canoe, with a head rest at one end and carrying knobs at each end. Most early wooden bathtubs (and their contemporary counterparts) are cooper's work, constructed like large barrels with staves and encircling hoops, or consist of multiple horizontal laminations that form the eventual shape. An example fashioned from a single large tree trunk is indeed a treasure. One should not lose sight of the fact, however, that mahogany was harvested through slave labor in the West Indies and Central America, lending a dark twist to bathing in this unusual object.

42 CRADLE
Portsmouth area, 1820–50
Painted basswood, birch, pine
H. 25½ in., W. 15⅜ in., D. 32¾ in.
Portsmouth Historical Society; Gift of Charles Hazlett (731)

This small cradle is notable for its unusual sleigh-type rockers that run in a front to back, as opposed to side to side, manner. Its painted decoration, including a red wash on the interior and a striped graining on the exterior, appears to be old and may be original. The cradle bears an old sticker reading "Hazlett / 6," indicating that it was number 6 on a list of objects given or lent to the Portsmouth Historical Society. It may have come from Charles Albert Hazlett (1847–1920), and it might be old enough to have been his cradle initially. Hazlett was a civic-minded banker and philanthropist, with a great deal of interest in historical subjects. He is known, among other things, for being the "pioneer wheelman" of New Hampshire; he began riding a bicycle in 1878.

43 CHILD'S TABLET-TOP WINDSOR HIGH CHAIR
New England, possibly Portsmouth, ca. 1840
Painted woods
H. 35¼ in., W. 16 in., D. 14½ in.
Portsmouth Historical Society; Gift of Mrs. James H. Dow

One English furniture scholar has labeled Windsor chairs as the "universal chair." Owned by rich and poor alike, used indoors and sometimes outdoors, the Windsor has been one of the most enduring chair forms since its introduction in the early eighteenth century. Almost always painted to mask their construction of various woods, each used for their particular properties, Windsor chairs have adorned many a parlor, porch, office, or restaurant. This child's high chair is representative of the common or garden variety expression of a specialized form. It has been painted top to bottom at least twice and has lost a footrest that was originally located a few inches below the seat. Although its early history is unknown, it came to the Portsmouth Historical Society from the Dow family.

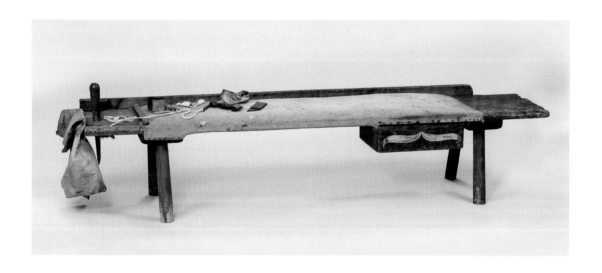

44 SAILMAKER'S BENCH
Probably Portsmouth area, 1860–65
Pine, cloth, mixed materials
H. 16½ in., W. 78 in., D. 16½ in.
Portsmouth Historical Society; Gift of Mr. Adams (655)

By tradition, this sailmaker's bench, with its canvas bag secured to one end, was used at the Portsmouth Naval Shipyard in the nineteenth century before its gift to the Portsmouth Historical Society, probably in the 1920s, from a Mr. Adams. It is shown here with a roping palm, a fid, a seam rubber, needles, and other tools of the sailmaker's craft drawn from the Society's collection. The only nod to decoration on this workmanlike object is the painted swag on the front of the small drawer housed at one end.

That drawer contains at least a dozen chalk and pencil inscriptions penned by a Frank Laskey and other men who used this bench as part of their daily life in the 1860s and 1870s. One is a biblical inscription, for example, while another records: "B. Johnson / of New York City / came to work at / Portsmouth Navy Yard / May the 20th / got kicked out February [?] / 25th 1868."

45A SWIVELING OFFICE CHAIR, ca. 1905
W.B. Moses and Sons, Washington, D.C.; retailed by Derby Desk Co., Boston, Massachusetts
Mahogany; metal base; replaced leather upholstery
H. 35 in., W. 22½ in., D. 19½ in.
Portsmouth Athenaeum

45B TABLE, ca. 1905
W.B. Moses and Sons, Washington, D.C.; retailed by Derby Desk Co., Boston, Massachusetts
Oak
H. 29¾ in., W. 49½ in., D. 30 in.
Charles B. Doleac Collection

45C ARMCHAIR, ca. 1905
W.B. Moses and Sons, Washington, D.C.; retailed by Derby Desk Co., Boston, Massachusetts
Oak
H. 39½ in., W. 26¼ in., D. 20½ in.
Charles B. Doleac Collection

These three objects are good examples of how furniture, even utilitarian factory-made
objects, can become tangible reminders of momentous events and important personages,

in this case the Russian-Japanese Peace Conference held in Portsmouth. The table *(cat.45B)* and swiveling armchair *(cat. 45A)* were used by Baron Komura, the head of the Japanese delegation, and bear inscriptions and a plaque, respectively, recording their use by him on September 5, 1905, when involved in the preparation and signing of the Treaty of Portsmouth that ended hostilities. The Portsmouth Historical Society has recently acquired a matching chair used by Sergius Witte, head of the Russian delegation. In 1905, "revolving" armchairs that could swivel and tilt were still something of a new phenomenon.

The oak armchair *(cat. 45C)*—reminiscent of the early banister-back chairs in this exhibition— is also associated with the peace negotiations and similarly was made elsewhere and imported into Portsmouth specifically for use in the process. Like all the furniture acquired for the meetings, the three pieces here were sold directly after the end of the conference by the Portsmouth Furniture Company. W.B. Moses and Son was a prominent establishment in the nation's capital from the mid nineteenth century until its dissolution in 1937. The White House and other branches of the federal government were among their many clients. All three objects are tangible reminders of the significance of this exceptional episode of civilian diplomacy that is one of nodal points of importance in Portsmouth's long history.

46 SIDE CHAIR
America, 1920s–1930s;
retailed by Margeson Brothers, Portsmouth
Painted wood, cane seat
H. 35½ in., W. 16¼ in., D. 17⅛ in.
Portsmouth Historical Society

In the 1720s and 1730s, Portsmouth's consumers could turn to local chairmakers to acquire seating furniture; several examples of those early chairs are included in this catalogue. Two centuries later, the same need was fulfilled by factory chairs made elsewhere in the United States and sold locally through retail stores. Inexpensive dining or kitchen chair were important furnishings in middle-class Portsmouth homes, such as those in the area known as Puddle Dock, during the middle of the twentieth century. This chair retains a fragment of a red and white printed paper label indicating that it was sold by Margeson Brothers, the prominent local furniture store operated by Richman Stanley Margeson (1902–1972) and Ralph Clyde Margeson (1905–1994). They maintained for many years a retail store on Vaughn Street and a warehouse on Albany Street.

Stylistically, this revival-style chair is in a popular mode that references different eras. It echoes the colonial period principally in its solid vase-shaped splat in the manner of a Queen Anne–style chair. The large rectangular crest rail, although it has shaped cut-outs on its lower edge, is more akin to Mission-style furniture of the arts and crafts period, while its straight tapered legs, trapezoidal seat, and straight stretchers recall federal-period examples. These chairs were often sold en suite with a large oval dining table, forming a constellation of objects used on a daily basis. These sorts of tables and chairs, largely ignored today by collectors, formed a significant part of the everyday life of many twentieth-century consumers, providing the means for them to gather for meals, conversation, and other forms of social interaction.

47 ROCKING CHAIR
America, ca. 1900;
retailed by Margeson Brothers, Portsmouth
Oak; leather upholstery; replaced leather seat
H. 42¼ in., W. 27¼ in., D. 33 in.
Portsmouth Historical Society;
Gift of Bob Shouse, 2014

This Mission-style rocking chair has two associations with the Seacoast area. Made at an as-yet- unidentified furniture factory, the chair, like much of the modern furniture in use in the area at the time, was retailed by Margeson Brothers of Portsmouth. It bears their label stenciled in black on the inside of the front seat rail on the removable slip seat.

More significantly, it also has a history of having been part of the furnishings of Rock Rest, a house at 167 Brave Boat Harbor Road in Kittery Point, Maine, now a landmark in the history of African American experience in the Seacoast area. Hazel and Clayton Sinclair of New York acquired this house in 1938 and began taking in guests during World War II. After expanding the house and renovating the garage, they operated Rock Rest from 1946 to 1977 as a summer retreat for an African American clientele, hosting as many as sixteen lodgers at a time. Rock Rest, now on the National Register of Historic Places, like similar venues throughout the country, provided safe and congenial lodgings for Black Americans before legal and de facto segregation ended in the United States. Through the efforts of historian Valerie Cunningham and the Portsmouth Black Heritage Trail, the Rock Rest archives are now permanently housed at the University of New Hampshire's Dimond Library. The site is featured in the Smithsonian's National Museum of African American History and Culture in Washington, D.C.

48 *JACK IN THE PULPIT* ARMCHAIR
Jeffrey Cooper (b. 1951)
Portsmouth, 2012
Cherry
H. 40 in., W. 23 in., D. 22 in.
Collection of the artist

Known especially for his carving and sculptural objects, Jeffrey Cooper works in Portsmouth and is the current chairman of the New Hampshire Furniture Masters Association. His training began on a commune in Oregon in the 1970s, and continued through study with Ken Harris at the League of New Hampshire Craftsmen, at the University of New Hampshire with Dan Valenza, and with additional study at Peter's Valley Craft Center in New Jersey and elsewhere (see www.cooperwoodsculptor.com).

Informed by his love of nature, evidenced here in the floral carving that adorns both the front and back of this side chair, Cooper's work is well-suited for the office, the home, and the garden. His carved animal benches in the Portsmouth Public Library, for example, delight that institution's many young visitors and are but one of his commissions for public seating in venues across the country. He was also selected to prepare the coffins that were used in the re-interment ceremony at the African Burying Ground in Portsmouth in 2015.

As a studio furniture maker creating "bespoke" work in a small shop, Cooper has much in common with his seventeenth- and eighteenth-century Portsmouth predecessors in the furniture trades, although his artistic vision and approach are contemporary. His work represents an option for today's consumers, particularly those who value individuality, artistry, and the hand of the maker.

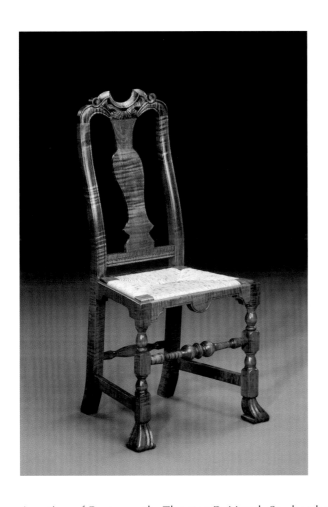

49 SIDE CHAIR
Thomas P. Hand, Sr. (b. 1949)
Rye, New Hampshire, 2017
Maple
H. 41 in., W. 19 in., D. 14½ in.
Collection of the artist

A native of Portsmouth, Thomas P. Hand, Sr., has been making high quality reproduction period furniture for the past forty years. Today, he works in a shop at his residence in Rye, crafting contemporary works in the various regional styles of colonial and federal America for customers and his own use (see www.thandperiodfurniture.com). Like the members of the Society of American Period Furniture Makers and many others, Hand enjoys developing a deep understanding of the materials and techniques used by eighteenth- and early nineteenth-century craftsmen. The recently completed chair shown here is an homage to the work of John Gaines III *(see cat. no. 19)*, the prolific eighteenth-century Portsmouth chairmaker. Although it is a meticulous reproduction in almost every detail, Hand increased the size of the seat rails by a modest amount to create a sturdier platform for modern posteriors.

50 POÄNG ARMCHAIR

Designed by Noboru Nakamura, ca.1976;
manufactured by IKEA (active 1942 to present)
Sweden, ca. 2015
Bent beech with walnut stain,
black leather upholstery
H. 37¼ in., W. 26½ in., D. 27½ in.
Private collection

Today, many consumers—especially millennials and others, perhaps a little older, setting up house, and including at least some in Portsmouth—seem to prefer the Scandinavian-modern-style furniture and household goods marketed by IKEA, the mammoth Swedish company. Because it comes in standard sizes and is produced in a manner that involves no "workmanship of risk," IKEA's "knock-down" goods can be ordered on-line with confidence. They are available at "affordable" prices and can be more or less easily assembled at home. As such, they stand at one end of a spectrum whose opposite end is typified by Jeffrey Cooper's chair *(cat. no. 48)* and Tom Hand's Gaines reproduction *(cat. no. 49)*.

The ergonomic design of this comfortable chair is given to a Japanese designer, Noboru Nakamura, who may have worked on it with Lars Engman of IKEA. It is based on much older designs from the 1930s by Alvar Aalto and others. Promotional literature issued by IKEA includes Nakamura's opinion that "A chair shouldn't be a tool that binds and holds the sitter. It should rather be a tool that provides us with an emotional richness and creates an image where we let off stress." According to Diana Budds (available online at https://www.fastcodesign.com/3063312/wanted/poaeng-the-little-known-history-of-ikeas-most-famous-chair, accessed January 16, 2017), the chair, originally known as the Poem chair, was first designed in tubular steel and re-modeled ca. 1992 to this wooden form. This example was acquired by a Portsmouth resident on August 2, 2015, for $168.94 ($50 for the frame and $109 for the "cushion," plus tax) at the firm's enormous store in Stoughton, Massachusetts. Ottomans and rocking chairs of the same general design are also available, and the Poäng line remains a bestseller for IKEA.

NEW HAMPSHIRE
Furniture Masters

FOUNDED IN 1993, the New Hampshire Furniture Masters Association has grown to become an organization of some two dozen artists dedicated to the fine art of furniture making. The founding members, including craftsmen and community leaders, wished "to build public awareness of New Hampshire's fine furniture makers and to cultivate an audience for their goods closer to home." Although many of the masters are from the Granite State, others hail from other parts of New England. For them, "building furniture is not simply a job, it is a way of life." Their outstanding work, known for its variety of traditional and innovative designs always expressed through excellent craftsmanship, is now in many museum and private collections. For more information, see www.furnituremasters.org.

As part of their educational mission, the group plays a vital role in a Prison Outreach Program in which selected inmates are mentored in woodworking techniques and create objects that are sold to the public through galleries and exhibitions. This innovative effort was started in 1999 at the Concord prison, and has subsequently broadened to include correctional facilities in Berlin, New Hampshire, and Maine. Ambitious efforts to expand the program even further are underway. The Masters also participate in the Studio-Based Learning Program, operated in conjunction with the American Furniture Masters Institute.

The NHFMA is an important organization within a regional and nation-wide network of individuals and groups dedicated to furniture. The Society of American Period Furniture Makers, for example, focuses attention on preserving and maintaining early designs and techniques, while the Furniture Society promotes all aspects of creativity in the furniture realm. The venerable League of New Hampshire Craftsmen and the Guild of NH Woodworkers are two of the other organizations that are active in this realm. All of these organizations, like the NHFMA, hold conferences and exhibitions, publish various materials, and do all that they can to educate the public about contemporary woodworking.

Detail above, Armchair by Jeffrey Cooper *(see cat. no. 48)*

Ted Blachly
Demi-lune table, 1998
Bubinga, East Indian rosewood
H. 33 in., W. 40 in., D. 17 in.
Photo: Dean Powell

Aurelio Bolognesi
Simple desk and cabinet, 2013
Quarter-sawn cherry, oil finish
Desk, H. 29 in., W. 30 in., D. 22 in.

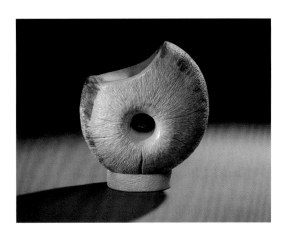

Jon Brooks
Torus chair, 2015
Pine, varnish
H. 26 in., W. 24 in., D. 18 in.

Greg Brown
Devil's Embrace, tilt-top table, 2014
Walnut, Claro walnut burl
H. 31 in., Diam. 33 in.

John Cameron
Crane armchair and side chair, 2015
White oak, horsehair
Armchair H. 40 ½ in., 19 ¾ in., D. 23 in.
Upholstery by Joseph Karagezian

Timothy Coleman
Heaven and Earth, 2012
English brown oak, English sycamore,
roasted ash
H. 50 in., W. 18 in., D. 14 in.

Jeffrey Cooper
Three Quotes from Ovid, 2013
Cherry, paldao veneer, roble burl veneer
H. 70 in., W. open 63 in., D. 2 in.
In collaboration with screen printer
Catherine Green

Michael Gloor
Windows sideboard, 2013
South American mahogany, frosted maple
veneer, ebony
H. 33 in., W. 48 in., D. 22 in.
Photo: Mara Trachtenberg

Garrett Hack
Va Va Vienna, 2011
Macassar ebony, cherry satinwood mother-of-
pearl, silver, bone, paint
H. 68 in., W. 26 in., D. 16 in.

Owain Harris
Ships in the Night, 2013
Poplar, Douglas fir, larch, holly, ebony,
varnish, wax
H. 16 in., W. 44 in., D. 17 in.
Photo: Charley Freiburg

David Lamb
Demi-lune table, 2015
Cuban mahogany, curly maple
H. 30 in., W. 36 in., D. 12 in.
Photo courtesy of the artist

Roger E. Myers
Side chair, 2014
Walnut, pine
H. 38 ½ in., W. 22 in., D. 18 in.
Photo: Lance Patterson

Richard Oedel
Jewel cabinet, 2014
Mahogany, Bird's-eye maple, cocobolo, 23k gold
H. 54 in., W. 28 in., D. 16 in.

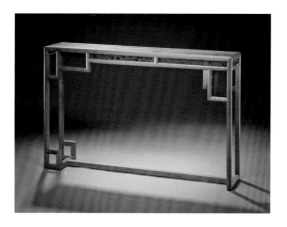

Brian Reid
Asia Moderne, 2012
Oak, walnut
H. 32 in., W. 60 in., D. 12 in.
Photo courtesy of the artist

Jeffrey Roberts
Newport Lowboy, 2015
Mahogany, pine
H. 36 in. W. 30 in., D. 20 in.
Photo courtesy of the artist

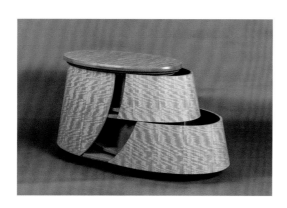

Brian Sargent
X and Why, 2014
Mottled Anigre, Swiss pear, hard maple
H. 19 in., W. 17 in., D. 17 30 in.

A. Thomas Walsh
Surf the Koa Wave side table, 2013
Koa veneer, South American and African
mahoganies, Macassar ebony; inlay and
details of curly maple, ebony, sapele, African
satinwood, and mother-of-pearl
H. 28 in., W. 22 in., D. 17 in.

Acknowledgments.

I AM INDEBTED in particular to Lainey McCartney, Curatorial Associate, and Hollis Brodrick. They have been co-curators at every step of the way, and this show would not have happened without their help in all its aspects. Lainey has kept track of the project and been a key contributor to the design and installation. Hollis, a tireless advocate for the show, contributed to the project in many ways, helping to locate objects, writing entries, and in general being a champion for the early material life of the Seacoast area about which he is so knowledgeable. Jeffrey Cooper, as the group's chair, was essential in coordinating the New Hampshire Furniture Masters part of the project, and we are grateful to him and all the Masters for making the contemporary component of this project possible.

Every member of the staff at the Portsmouth Historical Society, starting with Kathleen Soldati, has been extraordinarily helpful, patient, and cheerful as this project developed and came to completion. Richard Candee suggested the idea for this show several years ago, and I am grateful for his support and guidance.

The exhibition would not have been possible without the generosity of our public and private lenders; many are listed elsewhere in this catalogue, although some wish to remain anonymous. We deeply appreciate their willingness to let us borrow their favorite objects for several months. Many people at lending institutions have facilitated our requests and provided information, including Wes Balla and Doug Copeley, New Hampshire Historical Society; Elizabeth Akyroyd and Tom Hardiman, Portsmouth Athenaeum; Sandra Rux and Jeffrey Hopper, Warner House Association; Elizabeth Farish, Amanda Santoriello, and Rodney Rowland, Strawbery Banke Museum; and Barbara McLean Ward, Moffatt-Ladd House & Garden. Many other individuals also helped with this effort, including David McCartney, Valerie Cunningham, the Rotary Club of Portsmouth, Jon Winslow, S. Diego Rodriquez, Gary Sullivan, Matt Wajda, Jon Winslow, Alan Cutter, and Pat Wall. Brock Jobe's work on Portsmouth furniture has been an inspiration for this project, although he is not to blame for any of its contents. Jon Brandon of East Point Conservation Studio helped us make several of the pieces in the show look their best, Scott Cousins has taken care of moving and handling these fragile objects with his usual aplomb, and Nina Maurer, our guest registrar, has adeptly kept track of them all.

Most of the photographs here were taken by Ralph Morang, often under less than ideal conditions. It was a pleasure to work with Ralph as he inventively found solutions to whatever issues the situation presented. Susan Kress Hamilton of Phineas Graphics has made all our efforts look fantastic through her elegant design and typography. I am particularly grateful to Craig and Alison Jewett for their support of this publication. As young collectors of old material, they are helping to keep Portsmouth's longstanding involvement with furniture alive and well.

All photographs are by Ralph Morang, with the following exceptions:

Sandy Agrafiotis *(cat. no. 17)*
J. David Bohl *(cat. nos. 26, 27)*
Andrew Edgar Photography, Portsmouth *(cat. no. 49)*
Courtesy, New Hampshire Historical Society *(cat. nos. 14, 30A, 30B)*
Bill Truslow *(cat. no. 48)*
Blair Weaver *(cat. no. 6)*
Jon Winslow *(cat. nos. 15, 22, 24A)*

The photographs of works by the New Hampshire Furniture Masters are by Bill Truslow, unless otherwise noted.

BELOW: Detail, Armchair, England, 1680–90, Beech, H. 48¼ in., S.W.14½ in., S.D. 16¼ in., Strawbery Banke Museum; Gift of Old Colony Historical Society (1992.17). *(See cat. no. 3)*

A NOTE ON SOURCES

Much of what appears in this short catalogue is based on the research by several scholars contained in Brock Jobe, ed., *Portsmouth Furniture: Masterworks from the New Hampshire Seacoast* (Boston: Society for the Preservation of New England Antiquities, 1993). That book also contains a lengthy bibliography (pp. 441–47). We are indebted to all the good work contained in that volume, especially the essays by Brock Jobe, Jim Garvin, and Johanna McBrien. That catalogue did not deal with objects made or owned in this area after about 1825. The broader range of this exhibition is reflected in some works listed below.

Portsmouth Furniture and its predecessors were written before the days of the internet. Today, many institution's holdings and numerous other resources are available on-line. The journal entitled *American Furniture*, edited by Luke Beckerdite and published by the Chipstone Foundation of Milwaukee annually since 1993, contains many articles and book reviews of interest to the student of furniture in Portsmouth, only a few of which are noted below. Each issue also contains a bibliography of recent works on American furniture.

For many years, the New Hampshire Furniture Masters Association has published an annual volume devoted to the work of their members and to activities of the organization. Those have been an important resource; only two of the volumes are mentioned here.

The holdings of the Portsmouth Athenaeum—of books, manuscripts, maps, and other materials—and the Portsmouth Public Library are invaluable resources for any study of life on the Seacoast.

Bourgeault, Ronald. "Fifty Years of Antiquing in the Piscataqua Area." In *Piscataqua Decorative Arts Society: Volume 2, 2004–2006 Lecture Series,* 31–44. Portsmouth, N.H.: Piscataqua Decorative Arts Society, [ca. 2006].

Cooke, Edward S., Jr., Gerald W.R. Ward, and Kelly H. L'Ecuyer, with the assistance of Pat Warner. *The Maker's Hand: American Studio Furniture, 1940–1990.* Boston: MFA Publications, 2003.

Craig, James A. *American Eagle: The Bold Art and Brash Life of John Haley Bellamy.* Portsmouth, N.H.: Portsmouth Marine Society, 2014.

Cunningham, Valerie. "Rock Rest: African American Vacationing by the Sea." In *Cross-Grained and Wily Waters: A Guide to the Portsmouth Maritime Region,* ed. Jeffrey W. Bolster, 185–86. Portsmouth, N.H.: Peter E. Randall, 2002.

"Discovery: A Highly Important Chippendale Mahogany China Table." *Antiques and Fine Art* 16, no. 1 (spring 2017): 36.

Rock Rest, National Register of Historic Places nomination. https://focus.nps.gov/pdfhost/docs/NRHP/Text/07001449.pdf

Sack, Albert. "Tales of Portsmouth Furniture." In *Piscataqua Decorative Arts Society: Volume 1, 2002–2003 Lecture Series,* 30–40. Portsmouth, N.H.: Piscataqua Decorative Arts Society, 2004.

Safford, Frances Gruber. *American Furniture in the Metropolitan Museum of Art.* Vol. 1. *Early Colonial Period: The Seventeenth-Century and William and Mary Styles.* New York: Metropolitan Museum of Art, 2007.

Sullivan, Timothy M. "In Search of Robert Harrold, Portsmouth Cabinetmaker." *Warner House Newsletter* (winter 2001): 1, 4–5.

Trent, Robert F., Erik Gronning, and Alan Anderson. "The Gaines Attributions and Baroque Seating in Northeastern New England." In *American Furniture 2010,* ed. Luke Beckerdite, 140–93. Milwaukee, Wis.: Chipstone Foundation, 2010.

Ward, Barbara McLean. "Little Known Treasures of the Moffatt-Ladd House and Garden, Portsmouth, New Hampshire." *Antiques and Fine Art* (August-September 2006): 175–79.

Ward, Barbara McLean, ed. *The Moffatt-Ladd House: From Mansion to Museum.* Portsmouth, N.H.: Moffatt-Ladd House and Garden, 2007.

Ward, Barbara McLean, ed. *Produce and Conserve, Share and Play Square: The Grocer and the Consumer on the HomeFront Battlefield During World War II.* Portsmouth, N.H.: Strawbery Banke Museum, 1994. Distributed by University Press of New England.

Ward, Gerald W.R. "The Piscataqua on the Fenway: Portsmouth-Area Furniture in the Collection of the Museum of Fine Arts, Boston." In *Piscataqua Decorative Arts Society: Volume 1, 2002–2003 Lecture Series,* 51–56. Portsmouth, N.H.: Piscataqua Decorative Arts Society, 2004.

Ward, Gerald W.R., and Karin E. Cullity. "The Wendell Family Furniture at Strawbery Banke Museum." In *American Furniture 1993,* ed. Luke Beckerdite, 201-12. Milwaukee, Wis.: Chipstone Foundation, 1993.

Wright, Ursula, et al. *"We Tell Portsmouth Stories": Treasures from the Portsmouth Historical Society.* Portsmouth, N.H.: Portsmouth Athenaeum, 2004.

Volk, Joyce Geary, ed. *The Warner House: A Rich and Colorful History.* Portsmouth, N.H.: Warner House Association, 2006.

Doleac, Charles B., et al. *An Uncommon Commitment to Peace: Portsmouth Peace Treaty of 1905.* Portsmouth, N.H.: Japan-America Society of New Hampshire, 2005.

Garvin, James L. "New Hampshire as a Cabinetmaking State." In *Three Centuries of New Hampshire Furniture Making* (Concord: New Hampshire Historical Society; Canterbury N.H.: New Hampshire Furniture Masters Association, 1996.

Gronning, Erik K. "Late Seventeenth-Century and Early Eighteenth-Century Joined Furniture from Hampton, New Hampshire." In *Piscataqua Decorative Arts Society: Volume 3, Lecture Series 2007–2009,* 14–17. Portsmouth, N.H.: Piscataqua Decorative Arts Society, [ca. 2011].

Hardiman, Tom. "Theodore Atkinson's Journal and Conspicuous Consumption in 1730s Portsmouth." In *Piscataqua Decorative Arts Society: Volume 2, 2004–2006 Lecture Series,* 23–30. Portsmouth, N.H.: Piscataqua Decorative Arts Society, [ca. 2006].

Jobe, Brock. "A Portsmouth Settee at Winterthur." *Antiques* 151, no. 1 (January 1997): 184–87.

Jobe, Brock. "Two Case Studies: The Furniture of Portsmouth, New Hampshire, and Southeastern Massachusetts." In *Piscataqua Decorative Arts Society: Volume 2, 2004–2006 Lecture Series,* 62–64. Portsmouth, N.H.: Piscataqua Decorative Arts Society, [ca. 2006].

Kaye, Myrna. "Addendum: Discovering Portsmouth's Finials." *Maine Antique Digest* 22, no. 9 (September 1994): 11B.

Kaye, Myrna. "Discovering Portsmouth, New Hampshire's Premier Cabinetmaker." *Maine Antique Digest* 22, no. 7 (July 1994): 1B–4B.

Kaye, Myrna. "Evidence from Robert Harrold's Hand . . ." *Maine Antique Digest* 23, no. 8 (August 1995): 6B.

Kaye, Myrna, and Brock Jobe. "The Furniture of Robert Harrold." *Antiques* 143, no. 5 (May 1993): 776–83.

New Hampshire Furniture Masters Association. *Furniture Masters: Distinctive.* Manchester, N.H.: by the association, 2016.

"Portsmouth Peace Treaty, 1905–2005." On-line at www.portsmouthpeacetreaty.org.

Richards, Nancy, and Nancy Goyne Evans, with Wendy A. Cooper and Michael S. Podmaniczky. *New England Furniture at Winterthur: Queen Anne and Chippendale Periods.* Winterthur, Del.: Winterthur Museum, 1997.